Resource Book of Test Items

FOURTH EDITION

Biological Science
AN INQUIRY INTO LIFE

Prepared by the Biological Sciences Curriculum Study

Harcourt Brace Jovanovich

New York   Chicago   San Francisco   Atlanta   Dallas   *and*   London

Front cover: Doug Wallin/Taurus Photos

Printed in the United States of America

ISBN 0-15-360757-2

CONTENTS

Foreword

The high school biology programs developed by the Biological Sciences Curriculum Study consist of a textbook and laboratory activities, teacher's editions, and integrated materials, such as films, laboratory blocks, slides, research problems, and pamphlets. They offer a high degree of flexibility for design of curricular programs.

Teachers recognize that imaginative, inquiry-oriented, process-centered instruction can be vitiated by examinations that demand largely prosaic recall of specific information. Students are aware that examinations constitute their reward--in most cases a grade for classroom performance. If examinations ask mainly for lists of orders of insects, names of bones of the wrist, or simple recall of facts, students will concentrate on lists and facts. If examinations deal with the processes of science and the inquiry approach in a laboratory-oriented and open-ended manner, students will concentrate on these values.

In their awareness of these problems, teachers have requested that evaluation materials be made available. In response, the BSCS developed this book of test questions for *Biological Science: An Inquiry Into Life*. This current revision of the *Resource Book of Test Items*, keyed to the chapters in the 1980 edition of the Yellow Version, includes both factual, recall items and items dealing with higher categories of cognition. More than 1,500 multiple-choice items are included. Many of the items can be used to stimulate small-group interaction. These are designed to give the students practice in analyzing data and developing the mental tools of science.

In actual classroom experience, the items in this book have been found to be a valuable tool for evaluating students' biological understanding. This is not a book of tests but of test items. Feel free to pick and choose those that most closely parallel the objectives set for your course. The wide variety of items, in both content and difficulty level, allow you to tailor your examinations for specific student populations.

As always with BSCS materials, comments of users are earnestly solicited. We hope that this volume will be a valuable and useful adjunct to your biology teaching program. It will be made more so if you will communicate to us your experiences with its use, sent to the President at the address below.

Jay Barton II
Chairman of the Board of Directors
Biological Sciences Curriculum Study

Office of the President
University of Alaska
Fairbanks, Alaska

William V. Mayer, President
Biological Sciences Curriculum Study
Post Office Box 930
Boulder, Colorado 80306

Introduction

Biological Science: An Inquiry Into Life introduces students to the content and development of biological themes. All biology students should have the opportunity to employ the processes of science and should be able to demonstrate their understanding of basic biological ideas. Science is a noun representing *a considerable body of ideas and related facts.* Items that test students' retention of these facts are included in the "Information and Definitions" sections. Science also is the *process by which knowledge is gained.* Securing data on student progress in understanding science as a process requires a different kind of item. While the inquiry skills required to work with higher cognitive levels can be taught, it is much more difficult to assess a student's cognitive ability. The test items identified as "Application and Inquiry" will help you to evaluate inquiry skills. Both the recall and the inquiry items have been designed to help you evaluate the overall objectives of this program.

Students who have studied the Yellow Version should be able to

1. understand the biological ideas in each of the sections of the program.

2. recognize biological problems, formulate reasonable hypotheses, design experiments, and use experimental controls.

3. interpret data and modify interpretations based on new information.

4. use quantitative measurements when investigating natural phenomena.

5. demonstrate competence in laboratory skills.

6. show an interest in devising methods to solve problems and a critical attitude toward ideas that lack supportive data.

7. apply the contributions of biological investigation and science to problems facing the human species.

Student performance and the attainment of such objectives must be evaluated on more than the scores of examinations. Laboratory skills, ability to handle ideas, contributions to class discussions, creativity, and other such parameters are difficult to measure by paper-and-pencil examinations. However, these parameters must be considered as integral data contributing to the periodic evaluation of student progress. This resource book includes suggestions for the design of tests and for developing other means of gathering and interpreting data about student progress.

How to Use This Resource Book

This is not a book of tests. It is a source-book of test items. These items are designed to measure mastery of the materials in *Biological Science: An Inquiry Into Life.* Some are simple; others are complex. Some demand reading ability; others hold reading at a minimum. Some ideas are tested by more than one item, but if you will notice, these are phrased differently to appeal to different types of students. An essential purpose of this book is to help you recognize the kinds of test items that measure inquiry skills and the ability to use the processes of science.

The items in this book offer enough variety to allow you to pick and choose those that best exemplify the approach you have used. Use your objectives to select items that measure mastery

in those areas. There may be no questions that relate to your specific objectives; in which case the section on test construction (page viii) can help you construct your own.

The types of items included in the "Application and Inquiry" sections are a new experience for many students. Introduce them to these item sets through small-group discussion or homework assignments followed by class discussion. As students become more adept with these and you begin using them in tests, you might try the following: Give the students the introductory material plus any chart, graph, or diagram for the item set or sets before the test. This gives them an opportunity to practice analyzing the data and helps focus on process as well as on memory in reviewing for a test.

SELECTING ITEMS

You may want to cut individual items from the book and mount them on cards indexed by content. In this way items can be organized in a fashion congruent with your teaching style. Item cards then can be selected quickly to measure mastery of particular learning objectives.

Many questions are in sets that depend on a specific illustration or bit of information. These sets vary considerably in length and complexity. Use only those questions that apply to the ideas that have been considered in your course. An ideal selection of items would present a variety of formats to enable students to deal with ideas in several forms. The items for each chapter are arranged in two sections.

Information and Definitions. These items test students' ability to repeat or to use information and definitions.

For each recall question you select, include *two* that require students to apply knowledge or use inquiry processes. A recall item is exemplified by:

107. The rate of oxidation in living cells is controlled by the action of

    A sugars.
*   B enzymes.
    C fatty acids.
    D amino acids.

An item that tests students' knowledge is

108. Which of the following is an example of genetic inheritance?

*   A Matings of black guinea pigs and white ones produce all black offspring.
    B Animals lacking vitamin D have soft bones.
    C Children of athletes are usually good at sports.
    D Corn grown in a dry climate has small ears.

Application and Inquiry. These items test students' ability to apply principles and skills necessary for understanding biological problems and their ability to recognize and use processes of science. An inquiry process item is exemplified by asking students to interpret data or to draw conclusions from data. (*Note:* In the following item, interpretations concern the survival of nucleated and nonnucleated cell fragments as shown in a table.)

109. What is the best conclusion that can be drawn from this investigation?

*   A A nucleus normally is necessary for the continued life of the cell.
    B A nucleus is not normally necessary for the continued life of the cell.
    C Fragments of cells cannot live long.
    D The cytoplasm was altered when the nucleus was removed.

ADAPTING ITEMS

You may wish to alter the multiple-choice format to a form that best suits a particular group of students. For example, one of the multiple-choice questions has as its stem, "Which of the following best describes a mutation?" This is followed by four foils. The same question can be turned into a short-answer question by asking students to define a mutation or by rewriting, as, "A relatively permanent change in a gene is a _____." Multiple-choice questions also can be turned into a short essay by asking the student to "describe a mutation." Thus a variety of formats can be derived from multiple-choice items in accordance with your objectives.

However, do not assume that the complexity of a stem means a higher level of cognition. Many complex stems mask a pedestrian bit of information. Another factor to watch for is that of changing the cognitive category by a change in wording. Many questions that demand application or interpretation can be transmuted easily to items that require only recall if you add information or change wording. Many questions present the material of the book in a new setting or in a different fashion. These questions demand an application or interpretation of previously learned knowledge. Changing these items to reflect the way in which the material was presented will change the intellectual skills needed to solve problems or to apply inquiry abilities.

PREPARING TESTS

You have the permission of the BSCS to reproduce any items in this book for your classroom use. The copyright on this book, however, does cover reproduction of these items for any commercial use. The items you choose can be typed on ditto masters and the drawings and graphs can be traced. (A mimeograph stylus is especially useful for this purpose.) They can then be duplicated in class-size sets.

If you have a heat-sensitive duplicating system, you can copy the pages from the book and then cut out the desired items. Tape them directly onto a white sheet of paper to make a master. The question numbers and the correct-answer asterisks can be removed, and you can substitute your own numbering system. You may prepare an answer sheet or have students use a piece of paper that they have numbered.

A Context for Evaluation

For most students, the reward for accomplishment is a "good grade." They should not be deprived of this opportunity to realize success. But goals must be set that each individual can achieve according to his or her interests and abilities. Do not use the same meterstick to measure each student. You know your class and their individual strengths and weaknesses. Set your objectives accordingly.*

Test results must be viewed within the context of the total process of evaluation or their meaning is likely to be lost. If you establish valid objectives consonant with the skills and abilities of your students and if your tests measure these objectives, most of your students will be successful. When there is a significant difference between a student's test performance and your opinion of his or her ability, look seriously at your objectives, your methodology, or your evaluative devices.

Test scores will indicate areas that need to be retaught. Students should be aware that "missed ideas" will receive your attention also. Second or even third tests or quizzes should be given before grades are assigned. With analysis it will seldom be necessary to repeat the complete test. To encourage learning, select alternate items or tests with a varied format and give your students a second chance to correct missed ideas. Establish with your students the evaluative data base you will use to determine grades. Help students to see that this system encourages a maximum of success and that each member of the class can earn "good grades."

Use tests to evaluate your own performance and the adequacy of the materials. If, for example, many students missed an item covering an area you thought had been well developed, your reaction should be that either the materials or the teaching failed to illuminate the topic. Could the area have been approached in another way? Teachers using an examination to ask such questions of themselves will ultimately improve their teaching. Similarly, if students were exposed to certain materials and failed to achieve a given objective, could the materials have been at fault? If so, how could they be improved? Or, does a particular segment need more explication by you?

How you interpret test results hinges, in large measure, on the role you assign to testing in the total evaluation of learning. Testing may be thought of as sampling student responses to a set of stimuli--usually questions. Evaluation is a much broader concept.

*Material in this section is adapted from material by Bobby J. Woodruff, Ridgewood High School, Ridgewood, New Jersey, that appeared in the BSCS publication, *Testing and Evaluating Student Success with Laboratory Blocks*, 1969, D. C. Heath & Co., Lexington, Mass.

A useful way to think of evaluation is to consider it an interrelated process having three components. This involves three central questions for the teacher:

> What am I trying to do?
>
> How well am I doing it?
>
> How can I do it better?

The evaluation process can be expanded to the following questions:

What learning should be achieved by students?

To what extent are students succeeding in their learning?

How can more effective learning be realized?

How can the teaching-learning process be improved?

What higher-level goals are now in order?

The last question brings one back to the first question, and the cyclic nature of the evaluation process becomes apparent.

Securing a broad data base for evaluating students' progress is one of the most difficult and most important tasks facing any teacher. The task is difficult because the development of effective tests requires that the means and ends of the instruction program be kept constantly in view.

DATA BASE FOR EVALUATING STUDENTS

Once students feel confident when being tested, offer them different ways to communicate their progress. Tape recorders, films, overhead projectors, flannel boards, and graphing materials can be used effectively, as can group competitions and puzzles. Interest, enthusiasm, and work accomplished are indications of a genuine involvement that you should consider when you are rating students. To help establish a broader spectrum of data, ask yourself these questions frequently:

Do my students read and comprehend suggested reading material?

Do they notice related articles in newspapers or magazines?

Do they mention related television programs?

Do they anticipate laboratory sessions with eagerness?

Do they gain laboratory skills as the year progresses?

Do they come in at odd times to talk about science?

Do they bring in living materials to use in the classroom?

Does their readiness to enter into class discussions increase as the year progresses?

Does each individual get the opportunity to demonstrate her or his ability to inquire into problems?

Does their competency in discussing substantive ideas improve with time?

Can I find new ways to incorporate this spectrum of data into my evaluation of each student?

Inform students about the criteria you will use in the evaluation process and explain how the criteria will be weighed. The following suggestions are offered to assist you in collecting evaluation data.

- Duplicate a selected newspaper article or ask students to bring in one that presents a local view on issues related to conservation, ecology, public health, or general biology. Help students to analyze the article and recognize any biases. Have them suggest ways to check the accuracy of the article, alternative solutions to the problem or public action that might alleviate the situation.

- Divide the class into groups. Give each group the same discussion problems. Allow them time to read, discuss, and reach conclusions. Have one member of each group take notes on the remarks and conclusions offered. Circulate among the discussion groups. When you have allowed enough time for discussion, bring the class together. Have the reporter from each group present the group's remarks and conclusions. Help the class to realize how different groups can reach different but legitimate points of view.

- Consider criteria such as logical thinking, willingness to examine alternative explanations, and the formulation of sound hypotheses as a basis for evaluation. In these initial activities, adjust your expectations to experiences students have had. Reward them on this basis. Increase your expectations for clarity and precision as the year progresses.

- Show selected films with the sound turned off. Present the visual data in a way that elicits inquiry behavior and/or applications of knowledge. The BSCS Single Topic Inquiry Films can be used in this way. Groups of students can react to each inquiry posed in the films. The BSCS Inquiry Slides also can be used effectively for this type of evaluation.

ASSESSING LABORATORY ACTIVITIES

To assess laboratory skills, plan simple, interesting investigations that can be done in a series of short steps. These should be related to concepts the class has studied. You may want to put out all the necessary equipment or have students gather the equipment as part of the "test." Rate each student on how accurately and efficiently he or she accomplishes

each task. During the year, structure these performance or skill ratings so that you can measure the students' improved competency with laboratory techniques. As a review, periodically offer a laboratory practical test in which each student moves from one lab task to the next and records answers to simple and clear requests at each station.

Investigative laboratory activities are designed to provide students with experience in generating knowledge directly from nature. These activities demand a different type of evaluation. Provide students with opportunities to make conceptual statements based on observations of natural phenomena and to verify their interpretations through scientific procedures. This aspect of laboratory work also can be tested by a laboratory practical, by paper-and-pencil tests, and by observing and questioning the students as they work in the laboratory and the field.

Consider the English version of a laboratory practical on page ix. It was developed as part of the Matriculation Examination for BSCS students at the Israeli Science Teaching Centre, Hebrew University, Jerusalem. This example contains elements common to most BSCS investigations. A periodic check of these investigative inquiry skills will help your students place the laboratory activity in a proper perspective. You may find that students who do not do well on pencil-and-paper examinations can demonstrate logical insight when solving problems in the laboratory.

CONSTRUCTION OF TESTS

The multiple-choice format, which is used in this test book, is a versatile means of gathering data on student performance. Questions can be formulated on nearly any subject and the items can be designed to measure various levels of cognitive ability. (However, multiple-choice items that measure cognitive skills are the most difficult to construct.)

To assemble your tests from the resource book, first identify the objectives for which you wish to test. Next identify the subject-matter content and the cognitive ability levels required. Then select the appropriate items. Categorize each question carefully and analyze the level of cognitive ability required. See the BSCS *Biology Teachers' Handbook*, Chapter 3.* You may wish to write additional items to evaluate the material you covered more completely. Each question should be critically edited, and the item must actually test for the concept that you want to evaluate.

The following list of rules for multiple-choice items merits review periodically. Use these suggestions as guidelines to insure that you include relevant and dependable items in your testing program.

*BSCS, *Biology Teachers' Handbook*, 3rd ed., 1978, John Wiley & Sons, New York.

Laboratory Practical Problem

Measuring the Rate of Human Respiration

This setup consists of a 100-ml glass syringe attached to a 3-way valve by means of a tube with a clamp. The valve also is attached to a large glass cylinder containing a solution of N/10 NaOH with phenolphthalein as indicator. A rubber tube, attached to the valve, terminates in a small mouthpiece, which is used to blow expired air into the syringe.

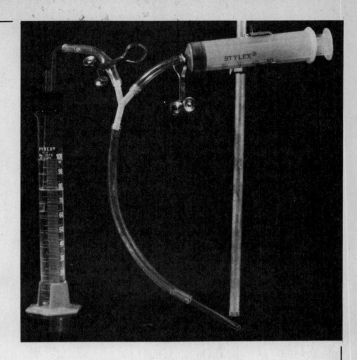

To the student:

1. Examine the experimental setup. Decide how to measure the percentage of CO_2 that you exhale. Do not do anything yet.

2. The following data will help you to understand how the system works.

   - 1 ml NaOH N/10 contains 4 mg NaOH.
   - This quantity combines with 4.4 mg CO_2.
   - 1 ml CO_2 has a mass of 2 mg.

3. Observe the system and answer the following questions.

   - What is the function of the syringe?
   - What is the function of the NaOH?
   - What is the function of the phenolphthalein?
   - How many mg of CO_2 are measured by this system?
   - How many ml of CO_2 are measured by this system?

4. Write, briefly, how you would perform the experiment. Show your statement to your instructor.

5. After approval, perform the experiment and write the results.

6. If you repeated the experiment 2 more times, would you get the same results in all 3 runs? Explain your hypothesis.

7. Test your hypothesis by doing the experiment. What are the results?

8. How can you intentionally change the results of the experiment? Explain your suggestion.

9. What are your conclusions from these experiments?

10. If a friend of yours performed the experiment, would the results be the same? Explain.

11. Disconnect the syringe from the system, using the clamp on the tube. Answer the following questions without performing any additional experiments.

   - Can you differentiate, using the small system, between 3 air samples: inhaled air, exhaled air, and residual air?

   - How would these 3 samples be different from each other?
   - How can you differentiate among them?
   - What variable is measured in this experiment?

Instructor's Guide: Testing Procedure and Evaluation of Responses

1. Check whether students understand how the system works and the underlying principle. Do this before allowing the students to start with the actual experiment by reading their answers to questions 3 and 4. When required, guide the students but take off credit in proportion to the amount of guidance supplied.

2. Students are expected to understand the need for several measurements because of two unrelated reasons: measuring errors and differences in the percentages of CO_2 caused by actual differences in the air samples.

3. The results can be altered in various ways; e.g., performing 20 knee bends or inhaling pure oxygen.

4. The answer to question 10 requires application of the results reported in answer 7.

5. In the last item, students are expected to propose distinguishing among the various air samples by the different percentages of CO_2. Since they are not allowed to use the graduated injectors, the best way to make the differentiation would be to measure the length of time for color to change (neutralization).

1. Ask first what is being evaluated.

2. Keep each item simple; avoid wordy, involved problems covering several concepts or principles and assorted biological data. Complex introductory statements (called *stems*) often obscure the actual inquiry skill that is being measured.

3. Fully identify sets of items where several questions refer to a single graph or diagram.

4. Use illustrations, graphs, or charts of complex problems only if several questions are asked. Justify the time required to interpret complex data.

5. The items should be unambiguous. The examinee should not have to guess the intent of the item writer.

6. Do not use a variety of synonyms in one item. Choose the term you used in the majority of cases in the classroom and stay with it throughout the item.

7. Always use *foils* (the multiple choices) that are plausible. One ridiculous foil reduces the advantages of multiple-choice items.

8. Construct foils that are parallel in construction and content.

9. The correct choice should always be unequivocally correct.

10. Avoid duplicate foils. For instance, if the keyed answer is "all of the above," you must expect that all others are correct answers. Avoid redundancy in the foils by including most of the information in the stem.

11. Avoid obvious clues to the right answer. Each foil should be about the same length and should avoid terms like "always," "never," and "all."

12. Avoid asking opinion questions such as, "What would you do in a given situation?" Any answer is acceptable.

13. There is little value in items that are difficult merely because the knowledge required is rarely mastered or because that knowledge is trivial.

ANALYSIS OF TESTS

Statistical analyses of objective tests are very useful in validating items and in looking at test scores for particular information about teaching and learning. For example, was the success of the students dependent on a cluster of items on which all students did very well? Did those students who had low total scores miss the same few items? You will find the following statistics necessary when you consider item data: number of students taking the test, class mean (average), range of test scores,

difficulty of each choice in each item, and discrimination index of each choice in each item.

The following paragraphs summarize the procedures for calculating descriptive and item-analysis data. If you desire more information on testing and evaluation procedures, the *Biology Teachers' Handbook* and a pamphlet by Educational Testing Service* are excellent sources.

The minimum number of students necessary for meaningful and valid item-analysis data is 20 to 30. The class mean and the range indicate general accomplishment and should be calculated for each test or examination. The mean is simply the sum of all students' scores divided by the number of scores. This can be expressed in equation form:

$$\text{Mean} = \frac{\text{sum of all scores}}{\text{total number of scores}}$$

For example, if a test were administered to ten students and their scores were 12, 12, 15, 9, 11, 10, 10, 16, 13, and 8, the sum of these ten scores would be 116. Dividing 116 by 10, the total number of scores, we obtain the figure 11.6, which is the class mean.

The range is simply the difference between the highest score in the class and the lowest. The highest and lowest scores are generally reported with this figure. In the above example, the highest score was 16 and the lowest score was 8, giving a range of 8 (16-8).

Since your instruction methods may vary in different classes, it probably would be more helpful to perform the item analysis separately for each class. You may, however, pool the answer sheets from one test that was administered to several classes. The following is a sequence that you can follow in calculating item-analysis data.

First, rank the papers in order from the highest to the lowest score. If you have pooled the answer sheets from several classes and the total number is quite large, take the top 27 percent and the bottom 27 percent of the answer sheets and randomly choose 50 papers from each group for the calculations. If the total number of answer sheets is between 50 and 90, the highest 25 papers and the lowest 25 papers can be used. If the total number of students is less than 50, the upper and lower halves can be used.

It is a good idea to use a single 4" x 6" card for each item, arranged more or less as shown on the following page.

For each item, tabulate the number of students in the High Group that selected each choice and record this on the card. Do the same for the Low Group. This can be done outside class by you or the students.

---

*Paul B. Diederich, *Short-Cut Statistics for Teacher-Made Tests*, 1973, Educational Testing Service, Princeton, New Jersey.

ITEM NUMBER   5. When a nerve connected to an isolated heart is
              stimulated, the rate of contraction slows. It
              is reasonable to conclude that the heart

          *(A) responds to nervous control.
           (B) requires nerve stimulation to speed it up.
           (C) is controlled by nerve stimulation only.
           (D) responds differently outside the body than
               in it.

Date used _____

ITEM DATA

	CHOICES			
	*A	B	C	D
HIGH GROUP	16	0	0	1
LOW GROUP	6	4	2	1
DIFFICULTY				
DISCRIMINATION INDEX				

DIFFICULTY

This is simply the percentage of students responding to each choice. To calculate the difficulty, divide the total number of students
responding to each choice (High Group plus Low
Group) by the total number of students responding. In equation form, this is:

$$\text{Difficulty of choice} = \frac{\begin{array}{c}\text{number of High-}\\\text{Group students}\\\text{who selected}\\\text{the choice}\end{array} + \begin{array}{c}\text{number of Low-}\\\text{Group students}\\\text{who selected}\\\text{the choice}\end{array}}{\text{total number of students}}$$

Consider the following data from a class of
30 students:

The difficulty for choice "A" would be

$$\frac{16 + 6}{30}, \text{ or } \frac{22}{30}, \text{ or } 73.3\%.$$

The difficulty for choice "B" would be

$$\frac{0 + 4}{30}, \text{ or } 13.3\%.$$

The difficulty for choice "C" would be

$$\frac{0 + 2}{30}, \text{ or } 6.7\%.$$

The difficulty for choice "D" would be

$$\frac{1 + 1}{30}, \text{ or } 6.7\%.$$

DISCRIMINATION INDEX

The discrimination index is the degree to which
the item discriminates between students in the
High and Low Groups. To calculate, subtract the
number of students in the Low Group responding
to a given choice from the number of students
in the High Group responding to that choice.
Divide this figure by one-half the total number
of students. In equation form, this is:

$$\text{Discrimination index of choice} = \frac{\begin{array}{c}\text{number of High-}\\\text{Group students}\\\text{who selected}\\\text{this choice}\end{array} + \begin{array}{c}\text{number of Low-}\\\text{Group students}\\\text{who selected}\\\text{this choice}\end{array}}{1/2 \text{ total number of students}}$$

With the use of the previous data,

the discrimination index for choice "A" would be

$$\frac{16 - 6}{15}, \text{ or } \frac{10}{15}, \text{ or } 0.67.$$

the discrimination index for choice "B" would be

$$\frac{0 - 4}{15}, \ -0.27.$$

the discrimination index for choice "C" would be

$$\frac{0 - 2}{15}, \text{ or } -0.13.$$

the discrimination index for choice "D" would be

$$\frac{1 - 1}{15}, \text{ or } 0.0.$$

A positive discrimination index indicates that more high-scoring students are responding correctly to that item than low-scoring students. A negative index means just the opposite. The completed Item Data Card for the question about nerve and heart function is shown below.

The class data indicate that this item was not difficult; 73 percent of the class marked the correct choice. In general, it was also a positive discriminator between students with top scores and those who did poorly on the total test. Most of the students who marked wrong choices on this item also had low scores on the total test. Apparently, few students in either group were fooled by choices C or D. Both of these foils should be examined and perhaps changed to make the item a bit more difficult.

A general rule of thumb is that an item with a Discrimination Index of less than 0.2 does not contribute to the test's reliability. If the index is higher than 0.4, that item contributes strongly to the reliability of the test.

Interpret item-analysis data cautiously. For example, an item may be relatively easy, with a difficulty of, say, 0.9. The item will not be a high discriminator. If that item measures a valid objective of your teaching, however, it should not be discarded.

We hope you will participate in our continuing efforts to improve this book by providing BSCS with information concerning your testing and evaluation programs. Copies of tests you have produced and used, and statistical data (for example, a copy of the 4" x 6" card for each item you have used) for such tests would be gratefully received if sent to Evaluation-Yellow Version, BSCS, Post Office Box 930, Boulder, Colorado 80306.

ITEM DATA	CHOICES			
	A	B	C	D
HIGH GROUP	16.00	0.00	0.00	1.0
LOW GROUP	6.00	4.00	2.00	1.0
DIFFICULTY	73.30	13.30	6.70	6.7
DISCRIMINATION INDEX	0.67	−0.27	−0.13	0.0

In Summary

Give tests immediately after a concept has been taught, when students are most likely to answer questions correctly. Short tests, as part of the lesson, give students a chance to use what they have just learned. This procedure gives them immediate satisfaction when they are right and immediate corrective feedback if they miss an idea. Each time, reinforce the learning by discussing each of the answer choices.

Every test should be a learning experience. Students are anxious to know how well they have done on tests. As soon as possible (the same period if practical), review the examination with the students. Discuss each question and encourage them to indicate why they gave the answers they did. When students have approached a problem logically and reasonably and have come up with incorrect answers, it may be more the fault of the test than the students. By reviewing questions when student motivation is high, the test becomes a learning experience rather than a grading one. Until the test has been reviewed with students, do not attempt to assign grades, if indeed a grade should be assigned at all. Give short tests frequently. Longer tests, given at infrequent intervals, leave no chance for remedial action when a topic is found to have been poorly comprehended. Apply an abbreviated statistical analysis of these tests. The difficulty and discrimination indexes can help you identify areas that need reinforcement.

Biological Sciences Curriculum Study

1 Biology—Investigating the Living World

INFORMATION AND DEFINITIONS

1. Much scientific knowledge has technological applications. Which of the following pairs is the best example of this?

    A The chemical structure of water: ice
*   B Patterns of inheritance: breeding of selected plants for crops
    C Wind patterns: air pollution
    D Insecticides: crop dusting

2. Science is a way of finding out about things. As such, it is

    A a precise, step-by-step process.
    B a way of collecting as many important facts as possible.
    C a search for evidence that will support a hypothesis.
*   D an attempt to find explanations for natural processes and events.

3. Quinine was discovered

*   A by accident.
    B after a long period of testing.
    C by making it in the laboratory.
    D by scientists studying heart attacks.

4. A person asks directions to a particular address. This person's *field of inquiry* is

*   A geography.
    B business.
    C language.
    D earth science.

5. Organisms of the same *kind* are said to be of the same

    A field of inquiry.
    B biology.
*   C species.
    D type.

6. A hypothesis is

    A true and acceptable.
    B a deduction.
    C a commonsense answer.
*   D a possible explanation.

7. The discovery of the cause of malaria was in part dependent on the development of

    A ways of draining swamps.
*   B the microscope.
    C quinine.
    D DDT.

8. It is now known that malaria is caused by

    A bad swamp air.
    B the bite of a mosquito.
    C drinking bad swamp water.
*   D a parasite in the bloodstream.

A number of control measures now prevent malaria from being transmitted from one human to another. The stages of the process of malarial infection are listed in the Key. Which of these stages is most affected by each of the following control measures?

KEY 1 Mosquito
      2 *Plasmodium* in the mosquito
      3 *Plasmodium* in the human
      4 Uninfected mosquito biting a human with malaria
      5 Infected mosquito biting a human

9. Draining swamps

*   A 1
    B 2
    C 3
    D 4

10. Quinine

    A 1
    B 2
*   C 3
    D 4

11. Pesticides

*   A 1
    B 2
    C 3
    D 4

12. Mosquito netting around sleeping quarters

    A 1 and 3
    B 2 and 3
    C 3 and 4
*   D 4 and 5

---

13. If we accept the hypothesis, "*Plasmodium* is the cause of malaria," which of the following deductions can we make?

    A *Plasmodium* causes diseases other than malaria.
*   B Everyone with malaria has *Plasmodium* in the body.
    C Eliminating marshes will eliminate *Plasmodium*.
    D Everyone who drinks polluted water will catch malaria.

14. The Romans did not know the cause of malaria. But they drained swamps because they observed that

    A people who drank swamp water caught malaria.
    B swamps gave off a bad odor.
*   C people living near swamps often caught malaria.
    D mosquitoes carried malarial organisms.

15. Redi put raw meat in open and closed flasks. Flies could enter the open flasks but not the closed ones. Worms appeared on the meat in the open flasks. No worms appeared in the closed flasks. This showed that

    A worms need only meat in order to develop.
    B an open container is better for worms because it receives air.
*   C flies could enter the open container and lay eggs.
    D spontaneous generation occurs under certain experimental conditions.

16. Spontaneous generation means that

  * A   organisms can originate from nonliving material.
     B   some organisms, like sea stars, can grow new arms or other missing parts.
     C   organisms can produce off-spring only of their own kind.
     D   some organisms resemble each other, like geese and bar-nacles.

17. Leeuwenhoek made the following statement about his discoveries: "This must surely convince all of the absurdity of these old opinions that living creatures can be pro-duced from corruption and putre-faction." How did he arrive at this opinion?

     A   By reading the writings of Aristotle and other scien-tists
  * B   After making careful obser-vations of microscopic life
     C   Through a series of carefully controlled experiments
     D   By analyzing the experiments of others and correcting them

18. Pasteur's experiments helped the advancement of modern medicine. These experiments showed that

  * A   microorganisms are carried through the air.
     B   spontaneous generation occurs only under controlled. con-ditions.
     C   sterile media may harbor microorganisms.
     D   flies do not lay eggs in a yeast infusion that has been boiled.

19. Suppose Pasteur had used a hay infusion instead of yeast, water, and sugar. He probably would have obtained some flasks with growth he did not expect. This would have happened because

     A   hay infusions are better food than yeast, sugar, and water.
     B   microorganisms will generate spontaneously in hay infusions.
     C   hay infusions can support life; yeast, sugar, and water cannot.
  * D   all organisms may not be killed when a hay infusion is boiled.

20. During his studies on spontaneous generation, Pasteur took his flasks up in the Alps. He wanted to expose them to the air at that altitude. He thought the air had

     A   less oxygen.
  * B   fewer organisms.
     C   no life-giving substance.
     D   less pressure.

21. After Redi completed his experi-ments on maggots and decaying meat, he studied a plant gall -- a swell-ing on the surface of a plant. Redi found a different type of maggot in the gall. He saw no way the maggots could have entered the plant stem. From this, Redi concluded that the maggots had developed spontaneously from substances of the plant stem. The conclusion that Redi made would

  * A   contradict his earlier work.
     B   support his original experi-ments.
     C   prove that spontaneous genera-tion occurs in plants only.
     D   definitely settle the problem of spontaneous generation.

22. The experiments of Pasteur demonstrated that

    A spontaneous generation cannot occur.
*   B arguments supporting spontaneous generation at that time were wrong.
    C further experiments on spontaneous generation were not necessary.
    D sexual reproduction is the only way new organisms can be formed.

23. Pieces of hay were soaked in a nutrient solution. Then the solution was boiled for ten minutes and was sealed from the air. A few days later the solution turned cloudy with bacteria. What is the most likely explanation for this result?

    A The bacteria were produced spontaneously from the solution.
*   B The solution contained bacteria that could survive boiling.
    C Boiling causes some bacteria to change into resistant forms.
    D Heating causes some kinds of bacteria to grow.

24. In an experiment, the condition that is different in each setup is the

*   A variable.
    B control.
    C hypothesis.
    D deduction.

25. The experimental setup that is used as a basis of comparison is the

    A variable.
*   B control.
    C hypothesis.
    D deduction.

26. A light microscope has a low-power and a high-power objective. One of the advantages of using the low-power objective is that

*   A a greater area of the slide can be viewed.
    B smaller objects can be seen.
    C the depth in view is less.
    D more detail can be observed.

27. Organisms seen under several magnifications seem to move at different speeds. Suppose an area is observed under high magnification. The field of view is

    A small, and the organisms seem to move slowly.
    B large, and the organisms seem to move slowly.
    C large, and the organisms seem to move quickly.
*   D small, and the organisms seem to move quickly.

28. Which of the following statements about science is *not* true?

    A Scientists are affected by their times, personalities, and friends.
*   B If two scientists draw different interpretations of the same facts, then some of the facts must be incorrect.
    C The principles of inquiry used in science are different from those used in other fields, such as history.
    D A hypothesis can be supported by a great deal of evidence but can never be viewed as a fact.

29. *Anopheles* mosquitoes are present in California, yet malaria is very rare. What is the most logical reason for this fact?

    A There are few swamps.
    B Most people include quinine in their diets.
*   C There are few malaria victims for the mosquitoes to bite.
    D Mosquitoes are confined to sparsely populated areas.

30. After a hypothesis is stated, the next logical step is to

    A define the problem.
*   B develop experiments and observations to test the hypothesis.
    C establish arguments for and against the problem.
    D accept or reject the hypothesis.

The next seven items refer to bubonic plague, or Black Death. This fatal disease is caused by a microorganism *Bacillus pestis*. It is found in rats and squirrels and is transmitted by fleas. Humans are highly susceptible to this disease and major outbreaks have occurred in the past.

In the fourteenth century, the plague killed almost half the population in Europe within two years. The plague returned in epidemic proportions every ten years or so until the last epidemic in 1665.

31. Which of the following in the plague cycle is similar to the mosquito in the malaria cycle?

    A Human
    B Rat
*   C Flea
    D *Bacillus pestis*

In order to protect themselves, people did a variety of things. Some of these were somewhat effective; some were not. Evaluate these behaviors according to the following Key.

KEY A Might decrease chance of getting plague
       B Might increase chance of getting plague
       C Would not affect chance much one way or the other

32. <u>C</u> Many refused to drink well water in the cities.

33. <u>B</u> Others gathered in the taverns.

34. <u>A</u> Many from the cities fled to isolated areas.

35. <u>B</u> Others locked themselves in cellars away from the light.

36. <u>C</u> Many consulted witches and witch doctors.

Bacillus pestis is present now in the squirrel population of the western United States. Over most of this area, the humidity is too low for fleas to survive. (Humidity is the water content of the air.)

37. Which of the following might cause an outbreak of plague among humans in the United States?

    A The growth of cities and towns in the west.
*   B Occurrence of a strain of fleas resistant to low humidity.
    C Transport of east coast squirrels to the west.
    D Increase in rat population in the west.

A customer presents a store clerk with a closed bag. The customer says, "This type of orange sells for 60 cents a kilogram." The clerk places the bag, unopened, on the scales and announces, "That will be 43 cents, please." The customer pays without hesitation and leaves the store. (An assumption is something one takes for granted without getting facts to support it.) Use the following Key to answer the next five questions.

KEY A An assumption made by the customer
     B An assumption made by the clerk
     C An assumption made by both the customer and clerk
     D An assumption made by neither customer nor clerk

38. __C__ The scales were in good working order and registered price and mass correctly.

39. __A__ The clerk read the scales correctly.

40. __C__ The other person is an honest person.

41. __B__ There are oranges in the closed bag.

42. __D__ Oranges are more nutritious than apples.

_____

(Note to teacher: This series may be used to evaluate Inquiry 1-1.)

The next five items refer to the following experiment. The experimental setup consisted of six test tubes, each containing red dye and a brass screw. The chart shows the results of a series of dye tests.

TUBE	MATERIAL ADDED	COLOR AFTER 30 MINUTES
1	Nothing	Red
2	10 glass beads	Red
3	10 sprouting beans	Yellow
4	Live cricket	Yellow
5	Breath, through straw	Yellow
6	Air pumped through dye	Red

43. The function of Tube 1 in this experiment is

*   A to provide a comparison for the other tubes.
    B uncertain when compared with the rest of the tubes.
    C to insure that there is an even number of tubes.
    D to provide an extra tube in case one is broken.

44. "A tube of dye will remain red if dead insects are placed in it." This statement

    A reports a result of the experiment.
    B makes an observation from the experiment.
    C states a conclusion of the experiment.
*   D makes a prediction from the experiment.

45. Suppose a live snail had been placed in Tube 4, rather than a live cricket. What would have happened?

*   A The results would have been the same.
    B The dye would have remained red.
    C The dye would have turned yellow but more slowly.
    D There is no way to predict the outcome.

In another experiment, three tubes of the dye solution were treated as follows:

TUBE	MATERIAL ADDED	COLOR AFTER 30 MINUTES
7	Distilled water	Red
8	Weak base	Red
9	Weak acid	Yellow

46. These three tubes suggest that the color change to yellow

    A indicates that there has been a temperature change.
    B results from sloppy experimentation.
*   C is due to the presence of an acid.
    D occurs whenever air is present.

47. Which of the following is a reasonable statement about the results in Tubes 1 through 6?

    A Living things raise the temperature of the tubes they are in causing a color change.
*   B Living things give off something that acts like an acid.
    C Given enough time, the dye in all the tubes will change from red to yellow.
    D Animals can change the color of a dye but plants cannot.

48. A scientist formulates a hypothesis, makes careful observations, and keeps accurate records of the findings. The scientist

    A usually finds data that support the hypothesis.
    B evaluates data, discarding those that do not support the hypothesis.
    C finds evidence that allows the hypothesis to become a theory.
*   D evaluates findings, alters the hypothesis, and tests again.

49. Some biologists isolate a pure strain of microorganism from the blood of a diseased cow. The biologists inject this microorganism into 50 cows; 40 get the disease. Which of the following conclusions is most reasonable?

    A The 40 cows have had the disease before.
    B The microorganisms do not cause the disease.
*   C The 10 healthy cows were not susceptible.
    D The microorganisms were too weak.

50. At one time, some people thought mice could arise spontaneously. They thought this would happen if dirty shirts and wheat grains were left in an open container for a period of three weeks. This idea might have been disproved by

*   A screening the container to keep mice out.
    B washing the shirts before putting them in the container.
    C applying logical reasoning to the problem.
    D sterilizing both wheat and shirts before placing them in the container.

A skin disease was found only in people who swam in a certain lake. The following four items are about this disease.

51. Parasites that live in a snail may cause this disease in people. The relationship between the snails and these people would be similar to the relationship between

      A people without malaria and *Plasmodium* parasites.

*   B mosquitoes and people with malaria.

      C *Plasmodium* parasites and mosquitoes.

      D people with malaria and people without malaria.

52. To find the cause of the disease, two water samples were taken from the lake. One was boiled; the other was not. One week later, drops of the two samples were placed on the skin of volunteers. None developed the disease. All the volunteers then went swimming in the lake. The skin disease occurred in 85 percent of them. Which of the statements below is most nearly correct?

*   A Lake water stored for one week does not contain the agent causing the disease.

      B Boiling can destroy the agent in lake water causing the disease.

      C A person will not contract the disease unless the whole body is exposed to the water.

      D A person must be exposed to the lake water over a long period of time to contract the disease.

53. Which of the following would support the hypothesis that snail parasites cause the skin disease?

      A Only one type of snail living in the lake had parasites.

      D Snails without parasites lived longer than snails with parasites.

      C Snail parasites were found on the skin of most people in the community.

*   D Snail parasites were found on all people with the skin disease.

54. A sample of the lake water was analyzed. It contained 17 kinds of microorganisms. How could you find out which one was the most likely cause of the disease?

      A Boil the water and test its effects on volunteers

      B Check the saliva of mosquitoes to see which microorganism is present

*   C Check the blood of people who have the disease to see which microorganism is present

      D Inject samples of the lake water into volunteers to see if the disease develops

_____

The next eight items are based on the following information and diagram.

Flasks 1 through 8 were half-filled with a liquid known to support the growth of microorganisms. Cotton stoppers were applied as indicated. Group I was treated no further. It was allowed to stand at room temperature. Group II was sterilized under pressure. Then it was placed next to Group I.

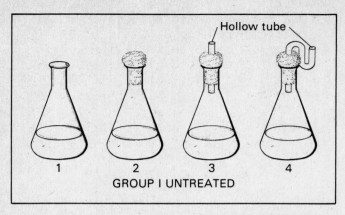

GROUP I UNTREATED

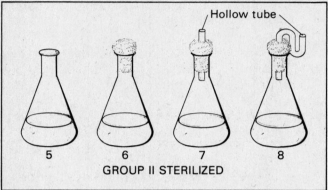

GROUP II STERILIZED

55. Organisms are most likely to appear first in Flask

*   A   5.
        B   6.
        C   7.
        D   8.

56. If all organisms are killed by sterilization, no growth should appear in Flask

        A   5.
*   B   6.
        C   7.
        D   8.

57. Suppose Flask 5 became cloudy before Flask 7. This probably would be due to

*   A   Flask 7 having a smaller opening to the outside.
        B   Flask 7 being heated for a longer time than Flask 5.
        C   no air getting into Flask 7.
        D   the broth in Flask 5 being contaminated before heating.

58. The hypothesis that all life comes from life would be supported if no microorganisms appeared in Flasks

        A   2 and 6.
        B   4 and 5.
        C   5 and 7.
*   D   6 and 8.

59. Spontaneous generation would be supported best if microorganisms grew in Flasks

        A   1 and 2.
        B   3 and 4.
        C   5 and 6.
*   D   6 and 8.

60. One hypothesis is that microorganisms only enter the broth from the air. This would be supported best if microorganisms grew in Flasks

        A   1 and 8.
        B   5 and 6.
*   C   5 and 7.
        D   6 and 8.

61. If microorganisms were found growing in Flask 2, they most likely

        A   arose spontaneously.
        B   came from air outside the flask.
*   C   were in the broth poured into the flask.
        D   were on the cotton stopper.

62. If microorganisms were found growing in Flask 7, they most likely

        A   arose spontaneously.
*   B   came from air outside the flask.
        C   were in the broth poured into the flask.
        D   came off the wall of the flask.

Four microscopes are set up in the laboratory to observe the same kind of microorganisms.

MICROSCOPE NUMBER	OBJECTIVE	OCULAR
1	10X	5X
2	20X	10X
3	40X	5X
4	40X	10X

63. With which microscope would you expect to see the fewest microorganisms?

    A 1
    B 2
    C 3
*   D 4

64. A slide containing microorganisms is examined with each of the microscopes. In which two microscopes will the microorganisms appear to move at the same rate?

    A 1 and 2
    B 1 and 4
*   C 2 and 3
    D 3 and 4

65. With which microscope would you expect to see the greatest number of microorganisms?

*   A 1
    B 2
    C 3
    D 4

2 The Molecules of Life

INFORMATION AND DEFINITIONS

1. Mechanists differ from vitalists in their approach to problems. Mechanists

    A make observations.
    B come to conclusions.
    C are concerned with life and matter.
*   D rely on explanation through testing.

2. Vitalism was Aristotle's philosophy that

    A humans are vital in the overall scheme of life.
*   B life is made possible by a force neither chemical nor physical.
    C knowledge of the physical world is vital to the concept, "Know thyself."
    D knowledge of one's self is the vital difference between human and animal life.

3. Molecules are combinations of

*   A atoms.
    B electrons.
    C bonds.
    D compounds.

4. In any compound

    A covalent bonds link atoms together.
*   B the number of each kind of atom is the same in every molecule.
    C atoms of one or more elements are bonded.
    D molecules show varying degrees of stability.

5. Lavoisier concluded that air is made up of two parts. He stated that one part will combine with phosphorus and the other will not. Which of the following experimental results best supports that conclusion?

    A About one-fifth of the air is oxygen.
    B The gain in mass of burned phosphorus always equaled the loss in air mass.
*   C No matter how much phosphorus was used, only a certain amount would burn.
    D As phosphorus is burned, it changes to a white powder.

6. Air is a

*   A mixture.
    B compound.
    C element.
    D molecule.

7. A theory is

    A a scientific fact.
    B a deduction.
*   C a hypothesis supported by much evidence.
    D a tentative conclusion.

8. If an atom gains an electron, it becomes an ion that is

*   A negatively charged.
    B positively charged.
    C not charged.
    D attracted to other similar ions.

9. An ionic bond is believed to be the result of

    A the actual sharing of electrons.
    B a release of energy.
*   C the transfer of electrons.
    D a combination of fats and proteins.

10. Which of the following equations indicates that an explosive reaction is possible?

    A $A + B \longrightarrow AB$
    B $AB \longrightarrow A + B$
    C $A + B + e \longrightarrow AB$
*   D $AB \longrightarrow A + B + e$

11. Which of the following is a good indication that energy is being added to a system?

*   A The temperature rises.
    B The temperature falls.
    C The temperature remains unchanged.
    D The temperature rises and falls.

12. Which of the following tools does *not* change energy from one form to another?

    A Windmill
*   B Electric transmission line
    C Engine
    D Generator

13. In 1828, Wohler synthesized urea in the laboratory. This was important because it

    A finally disproved the spontaneous generation hypothesis.
    B demonstrated the similarity between plants and animals.
    C was an important step in creating life in the laboratory.
*   D showed that living organisms were not necessary to synthesize organic compounds.

14. We say that chemical reactions waste energy. By this, we mean that

    A energy is completely destroyed.
    B pieces of chemicals break off and are removed.
*   C some chemical energy is lost as heat energy.
    D the reaction gets rid of a chemical it does not need.

15. Water is the best solvent known. This fact is important in living systems because

*   A in water many substances become separate molecules or ions that enter chemical reactions readily.
    B water ionizes readily, forming many hydrogen and oxygen ions.
    C water molecules prevent diffusion of small molecules.
    D the motion of water molecules increases as the temperature rises.

16. Carbon dioxide is classed as an organic molecule because it

    A is produced by organisms.
*   B contains carbon.
    C contains oxygen.
    D is necessary for plant growth.

17. Which of the following molecular characteristics would *not* be shown by the formula $C_6H_{12}O_6$?

    A Number of atoms
    B Kinds of atoms
*   C Position of atoms
    D Proportions of atoms

18. Starch and cellulose are compounds composed of many units of

    A amino acid.
    B fatty acid.
    C protein.
*   D glucose.

19. Protein molecules are built from

   A enzymes.
   B fatty acids.
* C amino acids.
   D glucose.

20. Which of the following procedures would inactivate an enzyme permanently?

* A Boiling the enzyme solution
   B Heating the enzyme to $21^{\circ}C$ and then filtering it
   C Filtering the enzyme out of solution
   D Diluting the solution with water

21. Two compounds have different chemical properties. But they contain exactly the same number of the same kinds of atoms. The differences between the two probably are due to the

   A sizes of the atoms.
   B masses of the atoms.
* C relative positions of the atoms.
   D numbers of electrons in the atoms.

22. Both iron filings and catalase can break down hydrogen peroxide. But catalase is classified as an enzyme and iron filings are not. This indicates that

   A iron filings and catalase act as catalysts only for this reaction.
* B iron filings are inorganic and catalase is organic.
   C iron filings and catalase have similar molecular patterns.
   D iron filings and catalase are used up in the reaction.

23. Which of the following is the most acidic pH?

* A 2.5
   B 4.0
   C 7.5
   D 9.0

24. At which of the following pH measurements is the solution most highly ionized?

* A 2
   B 5
   C 7
   D 8

APPLICATION AND INQUIRY

25. The great diversity of organic molecules or substances can be explained as follows.

   A There are only three basic elements used in forming all organic compounds.
* B Different arrangements of the same elements can produce totally different compounds.
   C Different arrangements are not as important as is the number of each of the atoms present.
   D Every type of compound requires different kinds and numbers of building blocks.

The next five items are based on the following experiment.

One part of Gas A was mixed with four parts of Gas B in a closed container. An electrical spark caused a violent explosion. Drops of liquid formed on the sides of the container.

After the explosion, two parts of Gas B were still present, but none of Gas A was present. The temperature of the container increased after the explosion.

26. The drops of liquid probably were

* A produced in a reaction between the two gases.
  B moisture from the air in the
  container.
  C an acid produced when the
  gases formed ions.
  D moisture caused by the spark.

27. The explosion indicated that

  A energy was needed to cause
  the reaction.
* B energy was released in the
  reaction.
  C matter was converted to
  energy.
  D energy was created in the
  reaction.

28. The remaining amounts of the
gases indicated that they

  A burned up in the explosion.
  B burned at different rates in
  the explosion.
  C reacted in a proportion of
  2 parts A to 1 part B.
* D reacted in a proportion of
  1 part A to 2 parts B.

29. The liquid in the droplets could
be represented by the formula

  A A-B.
  B A-A-B.
  C A_2B.
* D AB_2.

30. Which observation showed that
energy changed from one form to
another?

  A Proportion of gases in the
  container before and after
  the explosion
  B Formation of drops on the
  sides of the container
* C Explosion and change in temperature of the container
  D Need for electrical energy
  to start the reaction

The next four items are based on
the following investigation and information gained from the apparatus
shown below.

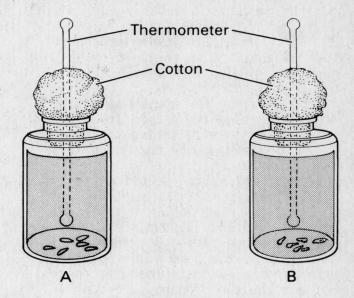

Sample A and Sample B were soaked
in water. Sample B was boiled in
water for ten minutes. Then, both
samples of wheat seeds were placed
in thermos containers. Thermometers
were inserted to record temperature
changes.

31. Which of the following hypotheses
could be tested with this design?

  A Soaking wheat seeds in water
  makes them sprout faster.
  B Sprouting wheat seeds give
  off carbon dioxide.
* C Sprouting wheat seeds give
  off heat energy.
  D Unboiled wheat seeds do not
  require oxygen.

32. The seeds were soaked to

  A adjust them to a constant temperature.
* B provide moisture to allow them
  to sprout.
  C wash off all contaminated
  organisms.
  D permit the water to absorb
  any extra energy.

14

33. If the temperature of the sprouting seeds increased, it would indicate that energy was being

    A received by the seeds.
    B released from the air in the container.
* C released by the seeds.
    D created.

34. Suppose the hypothesis was, "Boiling kills seeds and prevents them from growing." The best control for an experiment to test this would be seeds that were

    A boiled and soaked.
    B boiled but not soaked.
    C unboiled but not soaked.
* D unboiled and soaked.

_____

The next three items are based on the following investigation carried out under carefully controlled conditions.

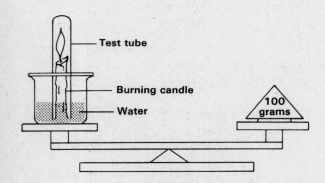

35. If no change in mass occurred as the candle burned, this would be explained best by

    A Dalton's atomic theory.
    B the law of conservation of resources.
* C the law of conservation of mass.
    D the law of conservation of energy.

36. At the end of the investigation, the materials on the left side of the scale would have a mass of

    A 20 grams.
    B 40 grams.
    C 80 grams.
* D 100 grams.

37. The amount of heat and light from the burning candle could be predicted best from

    A Dalton's atomic theory.
    B Wohler's synthesis.
    C the law of conservation of mass.
* D the law of conservation of energy.

_____

38. A phosphate ion (PO_4) has a charge of $^-3$. This means that the ion has

    A 3 more neutrons than protons.
    B 3 more electrons than neutrons.
    C 3 less electrons than neutrons.
* D 3 more electrons than protons.

39. Which of the following equations represents a reaction that could provide energy to a living organism?

    A A + B $\longrightarrow$ AB
    B AB $\longrightarrow$ A + B
    C A + B + e $\longrightarrow$ AB
* D AB $\longrightarrow$ A + B + e

40. A car burned a liter of gasoline in traveling 15 kilometers. What happened to the energy that was stored in the gasoline?

    A It was destroyed when the gasoline was burned.
* B It was changed to movement and heat.
    C It was released into the environment.
    D It was lost to friction between the tires and the road.

41. Which of the following is a molecule but not a compound?

*   A O_2
     B NO_2
     C $C_6H_{12}O_6$
     D CO

42. Which of the following is a statement that *cannot* be tested?

     A   Valves in the veins pre-
         vent blood from flowing
         backward.
*   B   A special force accounts
         for the flow of blood.
     C   Gravity affects the flow of
         blood in the legs.
     D   The heart pumps blood to all
         parts of the body.

43. Oxygen atoms are different from hydrogen atoms. This is because

     A   water (H_2O) is a combination
         of hydrogen and oxygen atoms.
     B   they have the same mass.
*   C   they have different masses.
     D   they react differently in
         gravitational fields.

44. Which of the following equations could be used to represent photosynthesis?

     A $A + B \longrightarrow AB$
     B $AB \longrightarrow A + B$
*   C $A + B + e \longrightarrow AB$
     D $AB \longrightarrow A + B + e$

45. Which of the following is a carbohydrate?

     A $CaCO_3$
     B C_4H_9OH
     C $CH_3(CH_2)_{12}COOH$
*   D $C_8H_{16}O_8$

46. Which of the following is *not* made up of glucose units?

*   A   Lipids
     B   Cellulose
     C   Starch
     D   Glycogen

The next three items refer to the following experiment.

One gram of freshly ground liver was placed in a test tube with 1 ml of hydrogen peroxide (H_2O_2). A gas formed in the tube. It was tested with a glowing splint. The splint burst into flame, identifying the gas as oxygen (O_2).

    Then, a gram of ground liver was *boiled*. When fresh hydrogen peroxide was added to the boiled liver, no gas formed. Ground liver treated with strong acid or base produced results similar to those obtained with boiled liver.

47. A hypothesis about enzyme activity in liver is being tested. The hypothesis is that this activity is destroyed by

     A   acids, bases, boiling, and
         hydrogen peroxide.
     B   acids, bases, and hydrogen
         peroxide.
*   C   acids, bases, and boiling.
     D   grinding the liver.

48. One of the test tubes was the control for these experiments. It was the test tube containing

     A   heated liver and hydrogen
         peroxide.
*   B   freshly ground liver and
         hydrogen peroxide.
     C   liver treated with base.
     D   liver treated with acid.

49. Suppose the substance that broke down the hydrogen peroxide were an enzyme. It could

    A not be recovered because it had been destroyed.
    B not be recovered because it was used up.
    C be recovered from the acid solution.
*   D be recovered from the liver after gas had formed.

———————————————

For the next four items, refer to the graphs of the activity of an enzyme.

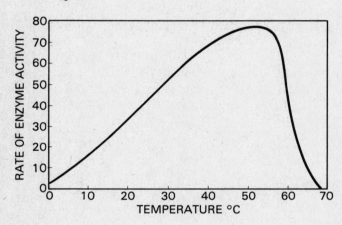

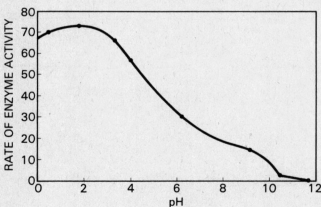

50. Enzyme X will work best in

*   A an acid medium.
    B a basic medium.
    C a neutral medium.
    D a carbohydrate medium.

51. The optimum pH for this enzyme is about

*   A 2.
    B 4.
    C 7.
    D 12.

52. Enzyme X will work best at a temperature of

    A 10°- 20°C.
    B 20°- 30°C.
    C 30°- 40°C.
*   D 40°- 50°C.

53. Enzyme X would be destroyed at a temperature of

    A 0°C.
    B 50°C.
*   C 75°C.
    D An enzyme cannot be destroyed.

———————————————

The next 11 items refer to enzymes. Use the Key to classify specific features or the way that they work.

KEY A True of known enzymes
       B True of some enzymes, not of others
       C Not true of known enzymes

54. <u>A</u> Are proteins

55. <u>A</u> Catalyze a specific reaction

56. <u>B</u> Are involved in energy-releasing reactions

57. <u>C</u> Act best at very high temperatures

58. <u>B</u> Are involved in synthesizing complex substances from simpler ones

59. <u>A</u> Act as organic catalysts

60. <u>A</u> Usually are not used up in a reaction

61. <u>B</u> Act at an optimum temperature of 37°C

62. <u>B</u> Act at an optimum pH of 7.5

63. <u>B</u> Are involved in breaking down complex substances to simpler ones

64. <u>A</u> Has a function determined by its chemical structure

---

67. Substance N probably is made up of

* A amino acids attached together in a definite sequence.
  B a nucleotide and a number of phosphates.
  C sugar molecules that will be used as an energy source.
  D fats and carbohydrates alternating in a chain.

The next three items are based on the following diagram of a chemical reaction.

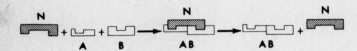

65. Which process is most likely to be illustrated by the diagram?

  A The breakdown of glucose to carbon dioxide and water
  B The formation of ADP from ATP with the release of energy
* C The action of an enzyme during the synthesis of a new substance
  D The release of energy from carbohydrates

66. After the reaction is complete, Substance N will

  A break down and be lost from the cell.
  B be used by the cell as an energy source.
* C combine with more A and B and repeat the reaction.
  D be stored by the cell for future use.

The next three items are based on the following graphs. In these graphs, the rate of enzyme activity is plotted against temperature and pH.

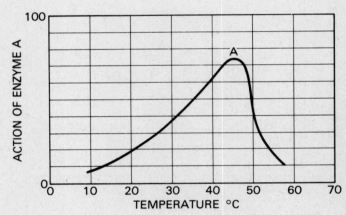

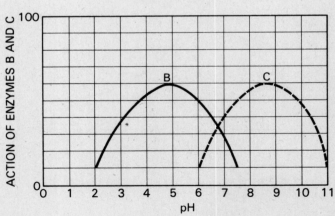

68. The graphs show that Enzyme C probably will be most effective

    A on the same substance as Enzyme B.
    B at 40°C and pH 5.
    C at a pH of 6.
*   D in a basic medium.

69. If Enzymes A and B are the same enzyme, at what temperature and pH would they be most effective?

*   A 45°C and pH 5
    B 30°C and pH 6
    C 40°C and pH 7
    D 50°C and pH 8

70. Which of the following would increase the amount of end product from the activity of Enzyme A?

    A Decrease in temperature from 30°C to 20°C
    B Decrease in the amount of material for the enzyme to act on
    C Increase in temperature from 40°C to 55°C
*   D Increase in the amount of material for the enzyme to act on

3 Cell Structure and Function

INFORMATION AND DEFINITIONS

1. The structure of a cell is closely related to its

      A age.
      B size.
*   C function.
      D movement.

2. Schleiden and Schwann observed that

      A all cells have nuclei.
      B cells do not arise from non-living material.
      C cells reproduce by an orderly process.
*   D plants and animals are made of cells and cell products.

3. Which of the following structures is present only in plant cells?

      A Cell membrane
      B Chromosomes
      C Cytoplasm
*   D Cell wall

4. A cell is from a photosynthetic plant if it has

*   A chloroplasts.
      B cell membranes.
      C nucleoli.
      D cytoplasm.

5. Robert Hooke coined the word "cell" from his observations of

      A the nucleus, cytoplasm, and cell membrane of animal cells.
*   B the empty cell walls of cork.
      C the nucleus, cytoplasm, and cell walls of cork.
      D the empty cell membranes of blood cells.

6. A theory differs from a hypothesis. A theory is

      A a guess that can be tested by experiments.
*   B a generalization that explains many scientific observations.
      C an experiment designed to provide evidence for a prediction.
      D a scientific fact that needs no supporting evidence.

7. Virchow's statement that "all cells come from other cells" is *not* consistent with

      A mechanism.
*   B spontaneous generation.
      C cell theory.
      D scientific observation.

_____

The next five items are based on the following cell diagrams.

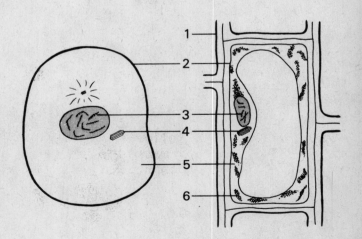

8. With Structure 3 removed, a cell could not

* A reproduce.
  B provide its own energy.
  C exchange materials with the environment.
  D secrete materials.

9. An organism whose cells have Structure 1 most likely is

  A dead.
  B large.
* C immobile.
  D small.

10. If Structure 6 is green, the presence of many of these allows the organism to

  A reproduce.
  B exchange material with the environment.
  C secrete material.
* D make its own food.

11. During cell division, some contents of Structure 3 would become visible as

  A Golgi bodies.
  B vacuoles.
* C chromosomes.
  D mitochondria.

12. Early cell theory includes the assumption that all cells have Structures

* A 2 and 3.
  B 2 and 4.
  C 3 and 4.
  D 4 and 5.

_____

13. In which of the following cubes would the movement of materials in and out be most efficient?

* A 1 cm
  B 2 cm
  C 4 cm
  D 8 cm

14. What is the surface area of a cube that measures 4 cm on each side?

  A 16 cm^2
  B 34 cm^2
  C 48 cm^2
* D 96 cm^2

15. What is the volume of a cube that measures 4 cm on each side?

  A 16 cm^3
  B 24 cm^3
* C 48 cm^3
  D 96 cm^3

16. What is the ratio of surface area to volume for a cube that measures 4 cm on each side?

  A 8:1
  B 4:1
  C 3:1
* D 2:1

17. Which of the following best explains why cells usually are very small?

  A The vacuoles in cells can hold only a limited amount of waste material.
* B Materials move in and out of small cells more easily.
  C Whenever a cell grows very large, it divides into two cells.
  D The cell membrane encloses the cell and prevents its growth.

18. A differentially permeable membrane is any membrane that allows the passage of

  A only small ions.
  B only water molecules.
* C some molecules but not others.
  D different molecules at different times.

19. Radioactive isotopes can be used as tracers. They are used to

   A fix and stain cells for observation with a microscope.
   B separate substances of different densities in a centrifuge.
* C see what cell parts are carrying out certain chemical reactions.
   D use a scanning electron microscope to look at thick specimens.

20. Three cubes of phenolthalein agar were soaked in sodium hydroxide. After ten minutes, Block A was pink all the way through. Blocks B and C were not. Which block(s) had the greatest ratio of surface area to volume?

* A A only
   B Both B and C
   C Either B or C
   D Impossible to tell from the information provided

21. A freshwater plant is put into a concentrated salt solution. The cells of the plant probably will

   A take in more fluid.
* B lose fluid.
   C show no effect.
   D take in salt.

22. A major function of the cell membrane is to

   A produce RNA for the ribosomes.
* B control what enters and leaves the cell.
   C hold adjacent cells together.
   D manufacture ribosomes.

The next four items are based on the following diagram of a cell.

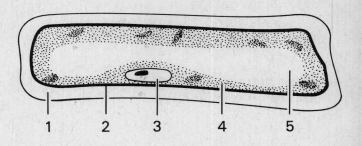

23. The chromosomes would be found in Structure

   A 1.
   B 2.
* C 3.
   D 4.

24. Which structures would be made of secreted nonliving materials?

   A 1 and 2
   B 2 and 3
   C 3 and 4
* D 1 and 5

25. Which structure controls the movement of substances in and out of the cell?

* A 2
   B 3
   C 4
   D 5

26. Which function is performed by Structure 1 in the diagram?

   A Movement
* B Support
   C Use of energy
   D Manufacture of food

27. Energy in the cell is released by the

    A   ribosomes.
    B   nucleus.
*   C   mitochondria.
    D   endoplasmic reticulum.

28. ATP is stored in the

*   A   mitochondria.
    B   ribosomes.
    C   Golgi bodies.
    D   endoplasmic reticulum.

29. The role of the ribosomes is to

*   A   assist in synthesizing proteins.
    B   pass on the hereditary materials.
    C   produce and release energy.
    D   manufacture food.

30. Which of the following has the greatest amount of available energy per molecule?

*   A   ATP
    B   ADP
    C H_2O
    D CO_2

31. Energy in burning systems comes from

    A   chemical reactions in which matter is changed into energy.
*   B   the rearrangement of chemical compounds into compounds with less energy.
    C   changing chemical energy into mechanical energy.
    D   combining atmospheric oxygen directly with starch or sugar.

32. Molecules of ATP

*   A   are all of identical chemical structure in all organisms.
    B   are found in cells of primitive organisms only.
    C   serve to pass hereditary information to the next generation.
    D   are very stable and thus are easily separated from cells.

33. During the process of glucose metabolism in the cell, there is a

    A   gain of hydrogen atoms.
    B   loss of ATP.
*   C   gain of ATP.
    D   loss of CO_2.

APPLICATION AND INQUIRY

34. Enzymes A and B change large carbohydrates to simple sugars in humans. Therefore,

    A   they also would change proteins to amino acids.
    B   the simple sugar would contain these enzymes.
*   C   they might be found in the digestive tract.
    D   they would be energy carriers for other reactions.

The following three items refer to this experimental setup:

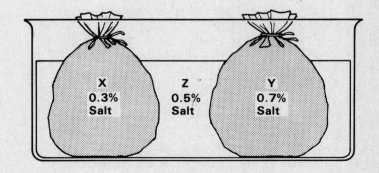

Two solutions of different salt concentrations (X and Y) are enclosed in bags made of a differentially permeable membrane. Both are immersed in a 0.5% salt solution (Z).

35. Water molecules will move from

* A X to Z and Z to Y.
  B Z to X and Y to Z.
  C Z to both X and Y.
  D X and Y to Z.

36. After enough time has passed, the salt concentration in Z will be

* A the same as X and Y.
  B greater than X and less than Y.
  C greater than Y and less than X.
  D greater than either Y or X.

37. The salt concentrations will change in X, Y, and Z. This is because

  A the membrane is permeable to salt but not water.
  B the membrane is permeable to water but not salt.
  C the salt moves from an area of higher to an area of lower concentration.
* D the water moves from an area of higher to an area of lower concentration.

The next nine items are characteristics of organisms. Decide whether each describes an animal or a plant cell. Use the Key.

KEY A Characteristic of an animal cell
     B Characteristic of a plant cell
     C Characteristic of either a plant or an animal cell
     D Characteristic of neither a plant nor an animal cell

38. _D_ At certain times, some slime molds form large masses that have many nuclei within a cell membrane.

39. _B_ At other times, each cell of the slime mold is surrounded by a cell wall.

40. _D_ The nuclear material of a bacterium is scattered throughout the cell; there is no nuclear membrane.

41. _B_ Most members of the genus *Euglena* have chloroplasts.

42. _B_ A bacterium is surrounded by a cell wall.

43. _C_ Within the nucleus of the single-celled *Euglena* is a nucleolus.

44. _B_ Blue-green algae are one-celled organisms or colonies of cells; the cells contain chlorophyll.

45. _A_ An ameba has a flexible cell membrane but no cell wall.

46. _C_ The nucleus of an ameba is surrounded by a nuclear membrane.

The next three items are based on an experiment on liver cells. The liver cells were ruptured and mixed in a test tube. This uniform mixture was then centrifuged. It produced four distinct layers of cell contents, as shown in the figure.

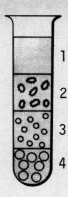

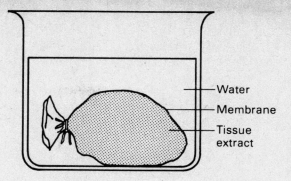

47. The material in Layer 3 contained a large amount of ATP. It probably was composed of

*   A mitochondria.
    B nucleoli.
    C cell membranes.
    D DNA.

48. The material in Layer 4 contained a compound of deoxyribose, carbon-nitrogen bases, and phosphate groups. This compound probably is

    A RNA.
*   B DNA.
    C ATP.
    D proteins.

49. The materials in Layer 2 were added to a solution of amino acids. Analysis showed the presence of protein fragments. The material in Layer 2

    A transmits hereditary charac-teristics.
    B supplies energy.
*   C synthesizes proteins.
    D breaks down fat.

The next ten items are based on the following information and diagram.

A biologist used the apparatus shown to separate molecules extracted from tissue. The biologist wanted to keep the enzymes that were responsible for digestion of starch inside the membrane. The membrane was immersed in water for a time. Then a sample was taken from inside the membrane. It was tested for the ability to cause digestion of starch. The test showed enzyme activity in starch digestion.

50. The biologist assumed molecular separation would occur because

    A water molecules would fill the membrane.
*   B the largest molecules would remain inside.
    C the smallest molecules would remain inside.
    D the membrane would absorb the molecules.

51. The decision to use a membrane to separate the molecules from the tissue was based on the fact that enzymes are

    A inactive.
    B organic molecules.
    C carbohydrates.
*   D proteins.

The biologist wanted to change the level of enzyme activity in the solution. She added the materials that had passed out of the membrane. Soon the enzyme activity rose sig-nificantly.

52. On the basis of the original hypothesis, adding materials that had passed out of the membrane should have

    A doubled the activity.
    B destroyed the enzyme.
*   C had no effect.
    D injured the membrane.

53. The biologist had assumed that the membrane did not allow the passage of enzymes. Thus, she could conclude that

    A water increases enzyme activity.
    B water decreases enzyme activity.
*   C other molecules may cause enzyme-like activity.
    D the original hypothesis was correct.

The biologist conducted a third experiment. She added *boiled* tissue extract to a membrane that contained enzymes with reduced activity. The level of activity of the enzyme increased.

54. This information indicated that the molecules responsible for the increase in activity were

    A mostly carbohydrates.
    B not fats.
    C mostly proteins.
*   D not proteins.

On the basis of the foregoing information, indicate whether each of the following statements is

KEY A supported by the data.
       B contradicted by the data.
       C neither supported nor contradicted by the data.

55. _A_ The tissue contained some molecules that were not changed by heat and were not protein.

56. _B_ Enzyme molecules alone catalyzed the reaction.

57. _A_ If the substances collected outside the membrane were boiled before they were added, they would still cause an increase in activity.

58. _A_ Addition of materials that had diffused into the water increased enzyme activity.

59. _C_ Addition of dilute acid increased enzyme activity.

_____

60. Which of the following observations supports the hypothesis that a nucleus is necessary to the life of a cell?

    A Animal and plant cells both contain nuclei.
*   B Removal of the nucleus is followed by death of the cell.
    C Some materials in a cell move back and forth through the nuclear membrane.
    D The nucleus of a cell divides before the material in the rest of the cell divides.

61. Suppose you were comparing chemicals from a green plant and an insect. Which of the following probably would be chemically different in the two organisms?

    A ATP
    B Water
*   C Enzymes
    D Glucose

62. A certain poison interferes with the formation of proteins. Which structure probably would be affected first by the poison?

    A Endoplasmic reticulum
    B Golgi bodies
*   C Ribosomes
    D Mitochondria

63. Suppose you dilute blood cells with water on a glass slide. As you watch through the microscope, the cells seem to explode. This probably is because you

```
*    A  used distilled water.
     B  used very salty water.
     C  added water too rapidly.
     D  used dead cells.
```

64. Cell M contains many more mitochrondia than Cell N. Which of the following is the most reasonable interpretation?

```
     A  Cell M is undergoing mitosis.
*    B  Potential ATP production is
        greater in Cell M.
     C  Cell N is producing more
        oxygen than Cell M.
     D  Protein production is higher
        in Cell N.
```

_____

Four principle tools or techniques are used to study cells. These are the compound microscope, biological dyes, chemical analysis, and the electron microscope. Assume that the order (in time) of uses of these tools is as listed in the Key below.

The next seven statements were made in the past or are acceptable today. In each case, certain tools or techniques had to be developed before these statements could be made. Select the tool that *first* permitted the statement to be made.

```
KEY  A  Compound microscope
     B  Biological dyes
     C  Chemical analysis
     D  Electron microscope
```

65. _B_ The nucleus contains threadlike structures called chromosomes.

66. _A_ The outer boundary of the cytoplasm is a continuous structure.

67. _A_ Within each cell is a single spherical structure, the nucleus.

68. _C_ One of the main components of the chromosome is DNA.

69. _D_ The endoplasmic reticulum connects the cell membrane with the nuclear membrane.

70. _D_ The channels of the endoplasmic reticulum are lined with spherical structures called ribosomes.

71. _D_ Cell parts, such as ribosomes, have internal structures.

_____

The next two items refer to the following investigation.

Cells were cut so that one fragment of each cell contained a nucleus and the other did not. The fragments with nuclei were separated from those without nuclei. From each group, 100 fragments were selected and placed in containers of nutrient medium under uniform conditions. The table indicates the results.

	NONNUCLEATED FRAGMENTS	NUCLEATED FRAGMENTS
INITIAL SAMPLE	100	100
SURVIVING 1 DAY	80	79
SURVIVING 2 DAYS	60	74
SURVIVING 3 DAYS	30	72
SURVIVING 4 DAYS	3	72

72. What hypothesis was being tested?

    A Any cell fragment will die
       eventually.
    B Twice as many cells will grow
       if each is cut in half.
    C The size of the cell fragment
       determines the amount of
       time it will live.
*   D A nucleus is necessary for
       the continued life of a cell.

73. Which of the following is a necessary assumption in this experiment?

    A The average size of the
       nucleated fragments was the
       same as that of the non-
       nucleated fragments.
    B More nucleated than non-
       nucleated fragments will
       live for three days.
*   C The same cytoplasmic materials
       were present in both kinds
       of fragments.
    D All of the fragments were
       of the same size.

Use the Key to identify each of the
following statements.

KEY A A restatement of the
        results
     B A logical interpretation
        of the data
     C The data show the state-
        ment is false.
     D An illogical interpreta-
        tion of the data

---

74. A The rate of dying in
        the nonnucleated frag-
        ments was greater than
        in the nucleated frag-
        ments.

75. A During the first day, the
        death rate was about the
        same for the two groups.

76. B Nuclei of the nucleated
        fragments that died in
        the first two days had
        been injured.

77. D Fragments of cells cannot
        live for more than four
        days.

78. C A cell or cell fragment
        dies as soon as the
        nucleus is removed.

79. A The percentage of non-
        nucleated fragments
        that died increased
        each day.

80. C The percentage of nucle-
        ated fragments that died
        each day increased after
        the first day.

81. B If the nutrient medium
        were adequate, the frag-
        ments probably would
        become complete cells
        that would live and
        divide normally.

82. B Normally, the nucleus is
        necessary for the con-
        tinued life of a cell.

---

4 Cell Reproduction

1. The part of the cell involved in transmitting hereditary traits is the

    A mitochondrion.
* B chromosome.
    C centrosome.
    D ribosome.

2. The chromosomes are largest and most easily seen when the amount of DNA is

    A lowest.
* B highest.
    C increasing.
    D decreasing.

3. The first indication that a cell is about to divide is the

    A disappearance of the nuclear membrane.
    B formation of chromosomes.
    C duplication of DNA.
* D division of the centrioles.

4. Meiosis is important because it

    A replaces dead cells in adult organisms.
    B doubles the chromosome number between generations.
    C produces a fertilized egg.
* D prevents increases in chromosome number between generations.

5. Which of the cells that make up the human body have 46 chromosomes?

    A All of the cells
* B The cells produced by mitosis
    C The cells produced by meiosis
    D The reproductive cells

6. When mitosis has ended, the number of chromosomes in each of the two new cells is

* A equal to the number in the original cell.
    B one-half the number in the original cell.
    C double the number in the original cell.
    D increased by two because of division of the centrioles.

7. Certain cells have twice as much DNA as other normal cells of the same organism. This is true of

    A cells that show a decrease in activity of the ribosomes.
* B cells that are in an early stage of mitosis.
    C a newly formed sperm cell.
    D an egg immediately after fertilization by a sperm.

8. Mitosis is important because

    A the new cell is the same size as the old cell.
    B each division produces four new cells.
* C the new cells have the same hereditary makeup as the original cell.
    D chromosome numbers are reduced by half in each new cell.

9. Dividing cells are animal cells if they have

* A centrioles and asters.
    B chloroplasts.
    C cell walls.
    D cell membranes.

10. An organism normally has 15 pairs of chromosomes. A biologist finds only 15 chromosomes in a cell from this organism. What is the most reasonable explanation for this observation?

    A A mutation has occurred.
    B The cell is dividing.
*   C The cell is a reproductive cell.
    D The cell is abnormal.

11. Mitosis is to growth as meiosis is to

    A energy production.
*   B sexual reproduction.
    C cell division.
    D movement.

12. In mitosis, one strand of each double chromosome goes to each of the resulting cells. This insures

    A reduction of chromosome number to one-half.
    B completion of the mitotic process.
*   C formation of new cells with identical DNA.
    D stimulation of cytoplasmic division.

13. The process of mitosis insures

    A unequal chromosome division.
    B reduction of chromosome number in new cells.
    C an increased chromosome number in new cells.
*   D equal division of nuclear materials.

14. Meiosis is to egg cells as mitosis is to

    A sperm cells.
    B replicated chromosomes.
    C homologous chromosomes.
*   D body cells.

15. The union of sperm and egg produces genetic information in the offspring. This information is

    A identical to that of one of the parents.
    B identical to that of both the parents.
    C different from that of either parent.
*   D a combination of that from both parents.

APPLICATION AND INQUIRY

16. Some cells have many nuclei. This could occur because

    A DNA does not replicate.
*   B cytoplasmic division does not occur.
    C chromosome strands do not move to opposite poles.
    D nuclear membranes are formed improperly.

17. The normal diploid number of chromosomes in corn is 20. The mature egg of a corn plant would have

    A 5 chromosomes.
*   B 10 chromosomes.
    C 20 chromosomes.
    D 40 chromosomes.

18. Which of the following theories is supported by the fact that a microorganism such as *Amoeba* divides?

*   A   Cell theory
      B   Theory of vitalism
      C   Mechanist theory
      D   Theory of spontaneous
          generation

_____

The next three items are based on the graph below. The graph shows the distance between paired chromosomes during mitosis as a solid line. It shows the distance between chromosomes and centrioles as a dotted line.

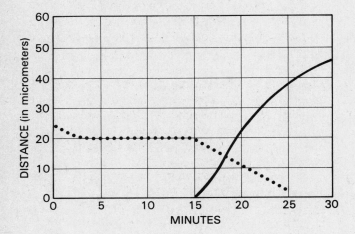

19. At what time did the chromosome pairs separate and begin moving toward the centrioles?

      A   0 minutes
*   B   15 minutes
      C   18 minutes
      D   25 minutes

20. At what time was the distance between the chromosome pairs equal to the distance between the chromosomes and the centrioles?

      A   4 minutes
      B   15 minutes
*   C   18 minutes
      D   20 minutes

21. Which of the following diagrams best illustrates the arrangement of chromosomes in the cell at 15 minutes?

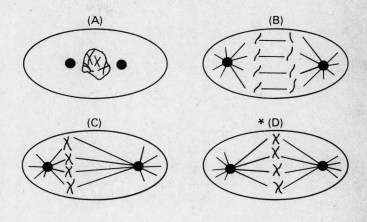

_____

Classify the next nine items using the following Key.

KEY   A   Mitosis
       B   Meiosis
       C   Both mitosis and meiosis
       D   Neither mitosis nor meiosis

22. __B__ The resulting cells contain one chromosome of each pair.

23. __B__ The resulting cells could be sperm cells.

24. __B__ This type of division prevents an increase in the chromosome number from one generation to the next in sexually reproducing organisms.

25. __A__ Each new cell contains the same kind and number of chromosomes as the parent cell.

26. __C__ A spindle forms in the cell.

27. __A__ Diploid cells are formed.

31

28. __B__ Monoploid cells are formed.

29. __C__ The nuclear membrane disappears.

30. __D__ The cell membrane disappears.

_____

The next three items are based on the following drawings. These drawings represent the overall process of one cell becoming two cells.

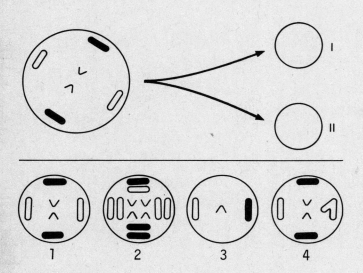

31. Suppose that Cells I and II are reproductive cells. Their chromosome pattern would be represented best by Figure

    A 1.
    B 2.
*   C 3.
    D 4.

32. Suppose the process being discussed is mitosis. Cells I and II would have a chromosome pattern as in Figure

*   A 1.
    B 2.
    C 3.
    D 4.

33. The figure that represents a cell that has failed to divide during mitosis is

    A 1.
*   B 2.
    C 3.
    D 4.

_____

The next four items are based on the following information and diagram.

Almost all of the DNA in a cell is located in the chromosomes. We should be able to predict a relationship between the amount of DNA and the appearance of the chromosomes during mitosis.

    The diagram shows changes in the amount of DNA during cell division. In each of the following items, relate the number on the graph to the stage of mitosis described. Read _all_ the items before you begin.

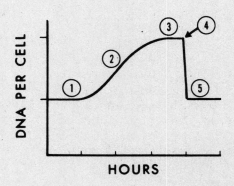

32

34. Chromosomes first become visible under the microscope.

       A 1
       B 2
*   C 3
       D 4

35. DNA and new chromosomes are being manufactured in the cell.

       A 1
*   B 2
       C 3
       D 4

36. The chromosomes have separated and the cell is dividing.

       A 1
*   B 3
       C 4
       D 5

37. The cell has just divided and each new cell has a full set of chromosomes.

       A 1
       B 3
       C 4
*   D 5

5 Patterns of Heredity

INFORMATION AND DEFINITIONS

1. The gene makeup of an organism for a particular trait is its

* A genotype.
  B phenotype.
  C dominance.
  D allele.

2. The appearance of an organism is its

  A allele.
  B dominance.
* C phenotype.
  D genotype.

3. What is the probability of a four appearing on *one* of a pair of dice rolled across a table?

  A 1/2
  B 1/4
* C 1/6
  D 1/3

4. What is the probability of two fours showing if a *pair* of dice is rolled?

  A 1/2
  B 1/6
  C 1/18
* D 1/36

5. Suppose that ten tosses of a coin all result in "heads." What is the probability that the 11th toss will be a "head"?

* A 1/2
  B 1/4
  C 0
  D 10/11

6. What characteristic of garden peas made them excellent material for Mendel's genetic studies?

* A Garden peas are self-pollinating.
  B There are multiple factors for a trait.
  C There are only a few genetic features to be studied.
  D Crosses between plants are not fertile.

7. Crosses between certain white- and red-flowered plants result in pink-flowered offspring. When these offspring are crossed, the ratio of plants expected is

  A all pink.
  B all red.
  C 1 red:1 white.
* D 1 white:2 pink:1 red.

8. Suppose Mendel grew pea plants from 32 seeds of a red-flowered F_1 plant and the first 18 plants to bloom had red flowers. What is the probability of red flowers on the 19th plant?

  A 0/4
  B 1/4
  C 9/16
* D 3/4

9. A cross is made between Aa and Aa. What is the probability that an offspring will have the genotype aa?

  A 1/16
  B 1/8
* C 1/4
  D 1/2

10. Three-quarters of the offspring from many experimental crosses showed only the dominant trait. The parents were

    A both pure dominant.
*   B both heterozygous.
    C one pure dominant, one recessive.
    D one heterozygous, one pure dominant.

11. What are the phenotypes of homozygous black and heterozygous black guinea pigs?

    A *BB* or *Bb*
*   B Black
    C White
    D Gray

12. Each parent contributes one of the genes for a particular trait. Whether or not the genes are exactly alike, the genes of the pair are called

    A variables.
    B hybrids.
*   C alleles.
    D gametes.

13. An individual has the genotype *Dd*. The reproductive cells it produces will be

    A 1/2 *DD* and 1/2 *Dd*.
    B 3/4 *DD* and 1/4 *Dd*.
*   C 1/2 *D* and 1/2 *d*.
    D 3/4 *D* and 1/4 *d*.

14. In a test cross, the organism to be tested is mated with one that is

    A heterozygous for the trait.
    B homozygous dominant for the trait.
*   C homozygous recessive for the trait.
    D of the same genotype as the organism being tested.

15. *A* represents the gene for a dominant characteristic and *a* is its recessive allele. If *Aa* mates with *aa*,

    A all offspring will be of the dominant phenotype.
    B all offspring will be of the recessive phenotype.
*   C 50% of the offspring will be of the recessive phenotype.
    D 75% of the offspring will be of the dominant phenotype.

The next five items refer to the following crosses.

P₁ CROSS	F₁ PLANTS	F₂ PLANTS
Round seeds X wrinkled seeds	All offspring round	5,474 round 1,850 wrinkled

Use this Key to identify the plants described in each statement.

KEY A P_1 plants
       B F_1 plants
       C F_2 plants

16. A Which generation is considered true-breeding?

17. B From the individuals of which generation did Mendel develop the idea of dominance?

18. C From which generation did Mendel develop the idea of the recessive trait?

19. A Which generation includes *no* heterozygotes?

20. B Which generation is 100 percent heterozygotes?

APPLICATION AND INQUIRY

The next four items are based on the following information:

In tomato plants, purple stems P are dominant to green stems p. Cut margins on the leaves C are dominant to smooth-edged leaves c.

21. A green-stemmed, smooth-leaved plant is crossed with a plant that is homozygous for purple stems and cut margins. What will be the phenotype of the F_1 individuals?

   *   A   Purple-cut
        B   Green-cut
        C   Green-smooth
        D   Purple-smooth

22. In the same cross, what will be the genotype of the F_1 individuals?

        A $PPCC$
    *   B $PpCc$
        C $ppCC$
        D $Ppcc$

23. Two plants of the genotypes $ppCc$ and $PpCC$ were crossed. No mutations occurred. What is the probability that they produced a green-stemmed, smooth-leaved plant?

    *   A   0%
        B   25%
        C   50%
        D   100%

24. A purple-stemmed, smooth-leaved plant was crossed with a purple-stemmed, cut-leaved plant. Among the F_1 offspring was an individual with green stems and smooth leaves. What must have been the genotypes of the parents?

        A $PpCc$ and $PPCc$
        B $PpCc$ and $PPCC$
    *   C $Ppcc$ and $PpCc$
        D $PpCC$ and $Ppcc$

For the next five items, use the following Key. Assume B = dominant; b = recessive.

KEY   A   All offspring will show dominant trait.
       B   All offspring will show recessive trait.
       C   About 50% of offspring will show recessive trait.
       D   About 75% of offspring will show dominant trait.

What will be the result if

25.   C Bb mates with bb?

26.   A BB mates with bb?

27.   B bb mates with bb?

28   D Bb mates with Bb?

29.   A Bb mates with BB?

For the next six items, indicate how many *different kinds* of reproductive cells (with respect to the traits listed) each of the individuals described could produce. Use the Key.

KEY   A   1
       B   2
       C   4
       D   8

30.   B   An individual with the genotype Bb

31.   A   An individual with the genotype $BBFF$

32.   C   An individual with the genotype $BbFf$

33.   B   An individual with the genotype $bbffMm$

34.   A   An individual with the genotype $bbffmm$

36

35. __D__ An individual with the genotype *BbFfMm*

_____

36. In the fruit fly, gray body *B* is dominant over black body *b*. Two gray flies were mated. They produced 158 grays and 49 blacks. The parents probably were

   A *BB* x *BB*.
*   B *Bb* x *Bb*.
   C *BB* x *Bb*.
   D *Bb* x *bb*.

37. Identical human twins were raised in different environments. They differed somewhat in intelligence. This shows that

   A heredity is more important than environment.
   B environment is more important than heredity.
*   C environment affects the expression of certain genes.
   D heredity controls the environment.

38. Genetic traits of certain seeds are: *L*, long, *W*, wrinkled, *Y*, yellow, *R*, ribbed; *l*, short, *w*, smooth, *y*, white, *r*, groved. Which of the following is the genotype for a short, wrinkled, yellow, grooved seed?

   A *llWwyyrr*
   B *LLWWyyRr*
   C *LlWwYYRr*
*   D *llWwYYrr*

39. A mother had Type-A blood. The father had Type-B blood. Their child had Type-O blood. It was apparent that

   A a mutation had occurred.
*   B the parents were both heterozygous.
   C the father was homozygous B.
   D the mother was homozygous A.

40. Two black, rough-haired guinea pigs were mated. Their offspring included six with black, rough hair and one with white, rough hair. We can assume that

   A one parent carried genes for white hair.
*   B both parents carried genes for white hair.
   C a mutation had occurred.
   D white hair is dominant.

41. *A* represents the gene for a dominant trait and *a* its recessive allele. If *Aa* mates with *aa*,

   A all offspring will be of the dominant phenotype.
   B all offspring will be of the recessive phenotype.
*   C 50% of the offspring will be of the recessive phenotype.
   D 75% of the offspring will be of the dominant phenotype.

42. A coin lands "heads" six times straight. What is the probability of "tails" on the next toss?

   A 100%
   B 60%
*   C 50%
   D 40%

43. Two coins are tossed together 40 times. How many times would you expect both coins to land "tails"?

*   A 10
   B 20
   C 25
   D 30

44. Two offspring resulted from the cross *Aa* x *Aa*. What is the probability that both offspring have the genotype *aa*?

*   A 1/16
   B 1/8
   C 1/4
   D 1/2

_____

The next two items refer to a breeding experiment with guinea pigs. In this animal, the gene for rough coat R is dominant to the gene for smooth coat r. A smooth-coated female is mated with a rough-coated male. She has seven smooth- and eight rough-coated offspring.

45. What are the genotypes of the parents?

    A Both rr
    B Both RR
    C Both Rr
*   D One rr and the other Rr

46. What are the genotypes of the rough-coated offspring?

    A All RR
    B All rr
*   C All Rr
    D 1/2 RR and 1/2 Rr

The next 11 items are based on the following diagram:

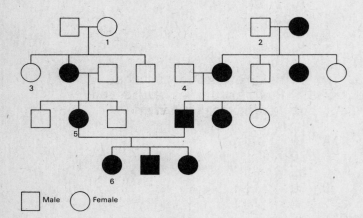

☐ Male   ◯ Female

The diagram is an example of inheritance of myopia (near-sightedness). Individuals with this condition are shaded; normal individuals are not. Use the Key to classify the items.

KEY A Heterozygous
        B Homozygous
        C Not enough evidence to determine condition

What is the genotype of

47. _A_ Individual 1?

48. _A_ Individual 2?

49. _C_ Individual 3?

50. _A_ Individual 4?

51. _B_ Individual 5?

52. _C_ Individual 6?

53. The gene that produces myopia is

    A dominant.
*   B recessive.
    C sex-linked.
    D lethal.

54. To Individual 5

    A each parent contributes a dominant gene.
    B one parent contributes a dominant and the other a recessive gene.
*   C each parent contributes a recessive gene.
    D The kind of genes contributed by the parents cannot be determined.

55. Individual 7 receives

*   A a dominant gene from the father and a recessive gene from the mother.
    B a dominant gene from the mother and a recessive gene from the father.
    C a dominant gene from each parent.
    D a recessive gene from each parent.

9. A color-blind man marries a normal woman whose father was color blind. The expectation would be that

* A 50% of their sons would have normal vision.
B all the daughters would be color blind.
C all the sons would be color blind.
D all the daughters would be carriers of the trait.

10. An organism with 12 chromosomes has how many linkage groups?

A 4
* B 6
C 8
D 12

11. People who have red hair usually have freckles. This can be explained best by

* A linkage.
B dominance.
C recombination.
D crossing-over.

12. Suppose we assume that "all trees have roots" and then say that "an oak is a tree." It follows that

A an oak is a tree.
B all trees with roots are oaks.
* C an oak has roots.
D all oaks with roots are trees.

13. In *Drosophila*, eye color is a sex-linked characteristic. Red eye is dominant over white eye. Which of the following would result from a cross between a white-eyed female and a red-eyed male?

A All red-eyed offspring
B All white-eyed offspring
C All females white-eyed and all males red-eyed
* D All females red-eyed and all males white-eyed

The next three items refer to this situation:

A woman's father had hemophilia. The woman does not have hemophilia. She marries a normal man.

14. What is the probability that their daughters will have hemophilia?

* A 0%
B 25%
C 50%
D 75%

15. What is the probability of hemophilia in their children?

A 0%
* B 25%
C 50%
D 75%

16. What is the probability of hemophilia among their male children?

A 0%
B 25%
* C 50%
D 75%

The next four items are based on the following information.

In cats, black coat color B is not dominant to yellow b. Heterozygotes Bb are "tortoise-shell" or "calico." The genes for coat color are carried on the X chromosome.

17. Assume that crossing-over or nondisjunction does not occur. If this is the case,

* A all calico cats are females.
  B all calico cats are males.
  C all offspring of a female calico cat are calico.
  D all offspring of a male calico cat are calico.

18. Suppose a female calico cat mates with a yellow male. What is the probability that one of the offspring will be calico?

  A 0%
* B 25%
  C 50%
  D 75%

19. In the same mating, what is the probability that a male offspring will be black?

  A 0%
  B 25%
* C 50%
  D 75%

20. In a cross of a black female and a yellow male,

  A all the female offspring are black.
  B all the male offspring are yellow.
* C all the female offspring are calico.
  D all the male offspring are calico.

The next two items are based on the following information.

In Dalmatian coach hounds, the desired breed has small black spots. Assume that a mating of small-spotted Dalmatians always produces some offspring with a solid coat, some with large black spots, and some with the desired small spots.

21. What is the probable genotype of the Dalmatians with small spots?

  A SS
  B ss
* C Ss
  D SSs

22. What cross probably would produce all small-spotted Dalmatians?

  A SS x SS
  B Ss x Ss
* C ss x SS
  D SS x Ss

The next six items are based on the following pedigree of a suspected sex-linked trait.

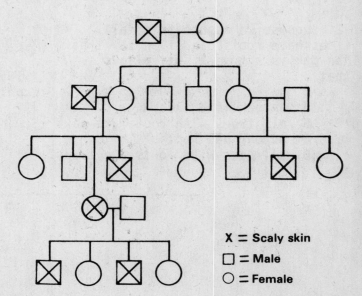

X = Scaly skin
□ = Male
○ = Female

Use this Key to classify the following hypotheses.

KEY A Supported by the data
     B Not supported by the data
     C Not related to the problem

23. <u>B</u> Scaly skin in males must
         be inherited through the
         fathers.

24. <u>A</u> Scaly skin in females
         must be inherited through
         both the fathers and the
         mothers.

25. <u>A</u> The trait for scaly skin
         is closely associated
         with the sex of the
         individuals.

26. <u>B</u> The inheritance of scaly
         skin involves one gene
         for the trait from each
         parent.

27. <u>A</u> The gene for normal skin
         is dominant to the gene
         for scaly skin.

28. <u>A</u> The gene for scaly skin
         is carried on the X
         chromosome.

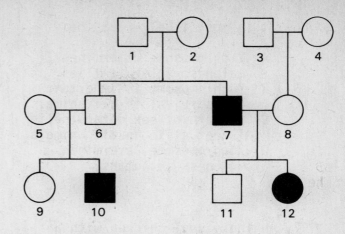

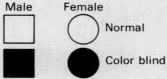

Male	Female
☐	○ Normal
■	● Color blind

29. <u>C</u> Individual 1

30. <u>A</u> Individual 2

31. <u>C</u> Individual 3

32. <u>A</u> Individual 5

33. <u>D</u> Individual 7

34. <u>A</u> Individual 8

35. <u>B</u> Individual 12

The next seven items are based on
the following chart. This pedigree
shows inheritance of color blind-
ness in humans.

Use the genotypes in the Key to
classify the individuals in the
following items.

KEY A *Cc*
     B *cc*
     C *CY*
     D *cY*

The next four items are based on the
following chart of chromosome
patterns in some animals.

CHROMOSOME PATTERN	FRUIT FLY	CHICKEN	HUMAN
X	Male		Female
XX	Female	Male	Female
XY	Male	Female	Male
XXX	Female		Female
XXY			

36. It is most likely that the

    A Y chromosome determines maleness in fruit flies.
    B Y chromosome is important for survival in all animals.
*   C pattern of sex determination is not alike in all animals.
    D X chromosome determines maleness in humans.

37. An individual chicken with a chromosome pattern of XXX most likely is a

    A female.
*   B male.
    C sterile male.
    D sterile female.

38. An individual with XXY chromosomes would be a male

    A if it were a fly.
*   B if it were a human.
    C under any circumstances.
    D under no circumstances.

39. What combination of chromosomes seems to determine sex in the fruit fly?

*   A Number of X chromosomes
    B Presence or absence of Y chromosome
    C Combination of X and Y chromosomes
    D Number of Y chromosomes

Use the Key to identify the relationships that exist between statements 1 and 2 in each of the five items below.

KEY A 1 (hypothetical statement) explains 2 (observational).
      B 1 (observational) is explained by 2 (hypothetical).
      C Both are hypothetical.
      D Both are observational.

40. _A_ 1. The hereditary factors are carried on the chromosomes. 2. An individual usually resembles the father about as much as it resembles the mother.

41. _B_ 1. A dihybrid test cross gave offspring ratios of 1:1:1. 2. Genes assort independently in the formation of reproductive cells.

42. _D_ 1. Egg cells are larger than sperm cells. 2. Sperm move by means of long tails; eggs have no method of movement.

43. _B_ 1. A dihybrid cross gives offspring ratios of 9:3:3:1. 2. Genes segregate at random in the formation of reproductive cells.

44. _B_ 1. Males of a certain insect have 11 chromosomes; females have 12. 2. In this insect, males will have fewer genes than females.

Use the following Key to indicate the most probable method of inheritance for the disorder described. Assume numbers of offspring large enough to indicate the pattern of inheritance.

KEY A Autosomal dominant
     B Autosomal recessive
     C Sex-linked dominant
     D Sex-linked recessive

45. _C_ All the female children of an affected male have the disorder; the males do not.

46. _A_ One-half of all the children of an affected male show the disorder.

47. _B_ All the children of two normal parents have the disorder.

48. _D_ Only the sons of two normal parents have the disorder.

49. _B_ The chances of an affected offspring from two normal parents is 1/4.

50. _D_ In this situation, a woman can be a carrier but a man cannot.

The next two items refer to Morgan's discovery of a male fruit fly with white eyes instead of the usual red eyes. He mated this fly with a normal, red-eyed female.

51. Assume that the gene for white eyes is recessive to the gene for red eyes. The F_1 generation should be

      A all white-eyed.
   * B all red-eyed.
      C 1/2 red-eyed and 1/2 white-eyed.
      D 3/4 white-eyed and 1/4 red-eyed.

52. A cross of two of the F_1 flies produced all red-eyed females and 1/2 red-eyed, 1/2 white-eyed males. How did Morgan explain this?

      A Genes are located on the chromosomes.
   * B The chromosomes of males and females are different.
      C Chromosomes and genes always occur in pairs.
      D The number of chromosomes in a reproductive cell is 1/2 the number in body cells.

7 The Hereditary Materials

1. A base becomes bonded to a sugar (ribose or deoxyribose). This in turn becomes bonded to a phosphate. The resulting molecule is called

* A a nucleotide.
  B an amino acid.
  C a bacteriophage. *a nitrogenous base*
  D an enzyme. *a nucleic acid*

2. The DNA molecule is described as a double-stranded, ladderlike structure. This structure was first suggested by

* A Watson and Crick.
  B Meselson and Stahl.
  C Beadle and Tatum.
  D Flemming.

3. The nucleic acid found in greatest amount in chromosomes is

* A DNA.
  B RNA.
  C ATP.
  D ADP.

4. If DNA replication is prevented, the process that is affected first is

  A energy production.
* B reproduction.
  C movement.
  D respiration.

5. When a virus infects a bacterium,

  A the entire virus enters.
  B only part of the virus protein enters.
* C only the genetic material of the virus enters.
  D the virus remains outside and digests the bacterium.

6. Which statement best describes the one gene-one polypeptide hypothesis?

  A Every gene requires a polypeptide to be active.
  B Polypeptides and genes are attached to each other chemically.
* C A single gene determines the formation of each polypeptide.
  D If a polypeptide is removed from a cell, it inactivates a gene.

7. Theoretically, DNA is most important in understanding living things. This is because DNA is a

  A spiral-shaped molecule made up of nucleotides.
  B complex chemical that is necessary for life.
* C carrier of genetic coding from parent to offspring.
  D part of the nucleus of cells in all organisms.

8. Before 1940, biologists thought that proteins were responsible for inheritance. They believed this because

  A living cells contain more protein than anything else.
  B proteins are made up of amino acids.
  C DNA is synthesized from proteins in chromosomes.
* D proteins are varied and complex.

9. A bacteriophage is made up of

   *   A an outer protein coat and an inner core of DNA.
       B DNA, RNA, enzymes, and a cell membrane.
       C a long, solid bar of lipid molecules.
       D all the parts of a typical cell except mitochondria.

10. The four nucleotides in a DNA molecule differ only in the

   *   A kind of bases they contain.
       B atomic structure of their sugar.
       C attachment of phosphates to the sugar.
       D position of their bases.

11. Genetic transformation in bacteria is caused by

       A mutation.
       B protein synthesis.
   *   C DNA.
       D heat-killed viruses.

12. Suppose the protein coat of a phage is labeled with S^{35} and the phage then infects a bacterial cell. Radioactivity will be found in

       A the bacterium but not in the phage offspring.
       B the phage offspring but not in the bacterium.
       C both the bacterium and the phage offspring.
   *   D neither the bacterium nor the phage offspring.

13. Assume that the DNA of a cell is 30% adenine and 20% guanine. Which of the following predicts the most likely percentages of the other bases in DNA?

   *   A 30% thymine; 20% cytosine
       B 20% thymine; 30% cytosine
       C 30% uracil; 20% cytosine
       D 20% uracil; 30% cytosine

14. Scientists thought that RNA might be the "messenger" that carries genetic information from the nucleus to the cytoplasm. Which of the following observations does *not* support that hypothesis?

       A RNA occurs both in the nucleus and in the cytoplasm.
       B When protein synthesis increases, movement of RNA from nucleus to cytoplasm increases.
   *   C A DNA segment controls the sequence of amino acids in a polypeptide chain.
       D RNA closely resembles DNA in chemical structure.

The next nine items are based on the following Key. Indicate which chemicals in a cell are directly involved in the process described in each statement.

KEY A DNA
      B RNA
      C Both DNA and RNA
      D Neither DNA nor RNA

15. _A_ The information to build a new individual is carried in sperm and eggs.

16. _B_ The coding mechanism moves between the nucleus and the cytoplasm.

17. _D_ Enzymes are necessary for most life activities.

18. _D_ Proteins are composed of amino acids.

19. _A_ The coding mechanism makes duplicate copies of itself.

20. _C_ It is involved in protein synthesis.

21. __B__ This is the messenger that transmits instructions.

22. __A__ The coding mechanism is found only in the nucleus of the cell.

23. __A__ Each coded instruction necessary for life in a new cell is the same as in the parent cell.

APPLICATION AND INQUIRY

24. A mutation occurs in a segment of a DNA molecule. It is reasonable to conclude that

    A enzyme synthesis is not affected.
    B protein synthesis is unchanged.
*   C the complementary RNA also would be changed.
    D the mutation is harmful to the organism.

25. Many ribosomes are found in cells in which

*   A large amounts of proteins are synthesized.
    B little energy is transferred.
    C rapid division is occurring.
    D there is a shortage of DNA.

26. Five events occurred in an algal cell:

    P An enzyme was manufactured in a ribosome.
    Q Cellulose was deposited in a cell wall.
    R Under the influence of DNA, a molecule of RNA was built.
    S A carbohydrate was formed.
    T A nucleic acid moved from the nucleus to the cytoplasm.

These five events are a cause-and-effect sequence. Therefore, the order in which these events occurred is

    A T-R-S-P-Q.
    B Q-P-S-T-R.
    C P-R-T-S-Q.
*   D R-T-P-S-Q.

The next nine items relate to the following data and Key.

The graph shows the production of certain chemicals in a cell. This production occurred during various periods before, during, and after mitosis.

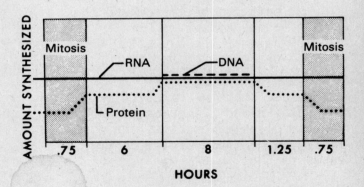

Use the Key to classify the statements.

50

A Restatement of the data
     B Logical hypothesis based
       on the data
     C Statement contradicted
       by the data
     D Insufficient evidence to
       evaluate this statement

SOURCE	QUANTITY OF NUCLEOTIDES IN DNA			
	Adenine	Thymine	Guanine	Cytosine
Calf	1.13	1.11	0.86	0.85
Rat	1.15	1.14	0.86	0.82
Moth	0.84	0.80	1.22	1.33
Virus	1.17	1.12	0.90	0.81
Sperm (of rat)	1.15	1.09	0.89	0.83

27. __A__ The amount of RNA being produced is constant.

28. __C__ Some DNA is produced at all times.

29. __C__ The amount of protein synthesis depends on the concentration of RNA.

30. __D__ Decreased protein is necessary for DNA synthesis.

31. __C__ DNA synthesis continues up to the beginning of mitosis.

32. __A__ The cell division cycle requires 16 hours.

33. __C__ During mitosis, metabolic activity of the cell stops.

34. __D__ After mitosis, DNA will be equally divided between the two new cells.

35. __D__ The synthesized protein would be found throughout the cell.

36. __C__ The DNA molecule is made up of nucleic acids, deoxyribose, and phosphoric acid.

37. __A__ Specific pairing of the nucleotide bases occurs in the DNA molecule.

38. __C__ The diameter of the DNA molecule is constant because of base pairings.

39. __B__ Adenine and guanine pair.

40. __B__ The ratio of adenine to guanine is fairly constant for all species.

41. __A__ The ratio of adenine to thymine is about the same in the sperm and body cells of a rat.

42. __B__ A cell always contains more adenine and thymine than guanine and cytosine.

The next seven items are based on the following Key and data table.

Use the Key to classify the statements.

A Supported by the data
     B Contradicted by the data
     C Neither supported nor
       contradicted by the data

The next four items are based on the following information.

Spores of *Neurospora* were X rayed. Different mutations seemed to affect closely related steps in a "chain" of chemical reactions. One such group consisted of compounds O, C, and A. Experiments revealed that

Mutant 1 would grow when any one of O, C, or A was added to the medium.

Mutant 2 would grow when either C or A was added to the medium.

Mutant 3 would grow *only* when A was added to the medium.

43. These data mean that each mutation was a change in

    A a single gene affecting two or more chemical products.
*   B a single gene controlling one step in a chemical synthesis.
    C several genes acting in a stepwise fashion.
    D two genes changing the synthesis of certain mutants.

44. What do the data indicate concerning the ability of Mutant 1 to grow? Mutant 1 is

    A unable to make O, C, or A.
    B able to make O if A is added.
*   C unable to change some prior substance to O.
    D unable to change some prior substance to C.

45. What do the data indicate about the ability of Mutant 2 to grow? Mutant 2 is

    A unable to make O, C, or A.
    B able to make O if A is added.
    C unable to change some prior substance to O.
*   D unable to change some prior substance to C.

46. What do the data indicate about the ability of Mutant 3 to grow? Mutant 3 is

    A unable to make O, C, or A.
    B able to make O if A is added.
    C unable to change some prior substance to C.
*   D unable to change some prior substance to A.

The next four items are based on the use of radioactive chemicals. These chemicals concentrate where stored or used in an organism. They can be detected because of their radioactivity.

47. To determine the rate of protein synthesis, what radioactive substances should be used?

    A Protein
    B Nucleotides
*   C Amino acids
    D Ribosomes

48. To determine the rate of DNA synthesis as distinct from RNA synthesis, what radioactive substance should be used?

    A Cytosine
    B Guanine
*   C Thymine
    D Uracil

49. To determine the rate of RNA synthesis, what radioactive substance should be used?

    A Cytosine
    B Guanine
    C Thymine
*   D Uracil

50. A nucleus containing radioactive chemicals is transferred to a non-radioactive ameba. The ameba with the new nucleus then has radioactive ribosomes in its cytoplasm. This is evidence in support of the

   A chromosome theory of inheritance.
   B existence of the DNA code.
* C functioning of messenger RNA.
   D one gene-one polypeptide hypothesis.

_____

The next four items are based on the following information and Key:

The following are messenger RNA codons for the amino acids indicated.

UUC - phenylalanine
AAU - asparagine
GUG - valine
AGU - serine

KEY A The transfer-RNA anticodon for phenylalanine-valine
      B The DNA sequence for phenylalanine-serine
      C The transfer-RNA anticodon for asparagine-serine
      D The DNA sequence for asparagine-serine

51. __B__ AAGTCA

52. __A__ AAGCAC

53. __C__ UUAUCA

54. __D__ TTATCA

8 An Analysis of Development

INFORMATION AND DEFINITIONS

1. One of Aristotle's ideas about development was called preformation. This idea said that the

    A differentiation of a structure requires the presence of another tissue.
    B embryo formation is controlled from the time of fertilization.
    C structures of the embryo are formed from chemicals in the egg.
*   D egg or sperm contains a new individual already formed.

2. The information necessary to produce an embryo is contained in the

    A nucleus of sperm only.
    B nucleus of egg only.
    C cytoplasm of both egg and sperm.
*   D genetic material from both sperm and egg.

3. Cell differentiation means that cells become different in

    A size.
*   B type.
    C location.
    D amount of DNA.

4. As a human becomes an adult, most cells stop dividing except in a few regions of the body. Some of these regions are the

*   A skin and tissues that form red blood cells.
    B heart and nervous system.
    C endocrine glands.
    D kidney and lymph system.

5. A cancer is caused by a

    A sudden change in the activity of a gland.
    B decrease in cell division.
    C change in metabolism of cells due to changes in hormone and food balance.
*   D sudden and abnormal increase in the rate of cell division.

6. The yolk of a chicken's egg is the

    A size to which the embryo will grow before hatching.
*   B food supply for the developing chick.
    C size of excretory material the chick will produce before hatching.
    D surface that the embryo uses to shape its body form.

7. In the developing chick, the allantois functions as

    A a respiratory organ.
*   B an excretory organ.
    C a digestive organ.
    D a circulatory organ.

8. The amnion of the chick functions in

*   A protecting the developing chick.
    B storing excretory materials.
    C providing nourishment for the chick.
    D stimulating the proper sequence of developmental stages.

9. The zygote is a single cell containing

    A two nuclei.
    B chromosomes of only the female parent.
* C chromosomes of both the sperm and the egg.
    D one nucleus and a monoploid set of chromosomes.

10. Differentiation of cells involves

    A increase in size.
    B production of more cells.
* C various types of cells.
    D movement of cells.

11. In some organisms, an embryo develops in an egg outside the mother's body. The eggs contain stored food to last until the

    A sperm fertilizes the egg.
    B zygote begins to divide.
    C embryo develops a circulatory system.
* D new organism can get food on its own.

12. The Jacob-Monod model provides a good explanation of how

    A proteins are synthesized from the DNA code.
    B genetic information passes from parents to offspring.
* C genes become active or inactive during development.
    D tissues differentiate through embryonic induction.

13. Different kinds of tissue are produced in a zygote. This process is called

    A preformation.
    B regeneration.
    C cleavage.
* D differentiation.

14. In frog development, the stage at which the embryo is a fluid-filled, hollow ball is called the

    A blastopore.
    B gastrula.
    C chorion.
* D blastula.

15. The outer layer of cells of the gastrula is called the

* A ectoderm.
    B mesoderm.
    C endoderm.
    D gastroderm.

16. Which of the following is an organ?

    A Red blood cell
* B Heart
    C Digestive system
    D Bone marrow

17. One of the results of failure to replace cells is

    A decrease in size.
* B aging.
    C cancer.
    D mitosis ceases.

APPLICATION AND INQUIRY

The next three items are based on the following experiment.

Two petri dishes contain physiological saline solution. Mesoderm is placed in Dish A for 3 hours and then is removed. Then ectoderm is placed in both Dishes A and B.

18. Initiation of differentiation is best explained by

    A preformation.
* B embryonic induction.
    C regeneration.
    D cytoplasmic inheritance.

19. Which of the following is the most precise statement of the hypothesis this experiment was testing?

    A Mesoderm causes some changes in ectoderm that can be seen.
    B Both ectoderm and mesoderm are necessary for cell differentiation.
    C Mesoderm is formed from undifferentiated tissues in the embryo.
*   D Mesoderm produces a chemical that induces ectoderm to differentiate.

20. In this experiment, which of the following results would most likely occur?

    A Ectoderm in both Dishes A and B would differentiate.
    B Ectoderm in both Dishes A and B would grow but not differentiate.
    C Ectoderm would differentiate In Dish B but not in Dish A.
*   D Ectoderm would differentiate in Dish A but not in Dish B.

---

21. Preformation may still be a valid hypothesis if one considers the preformed package to be

    A in either the egg or sperm.
    B in the sperm only.
    C in the egg only.
*   D in both the egg and sperm.

The next 21 items are based on the following material concerning salamander development.

Preliminary information. Salamander eggs in ponds do not hatch unless they are fertilized by sperm. Sperm cells alone do not develop into adults.

Use the Key to classify the following statements.

KEY A Hypothesis consistent with the data
       B Hypothesis contrary to the data
       C Insufficient evidence to evaluate the hypothesis
       D Restatement of the data

22. _C_ Cytoplasm is necessary for the development of a cell into an adult.

23. _D_ A sperm nucleus alone does not normally produce an adult.

24. _A_ Both egg and sperm are necessary to form a zygote that develops into an adult.

25. _B_ Eggs can hatch without the action of the sperm.

26. _C_ Temperature is an important control on the hatching of salamander eggs.

27. _D_ Fertilization is necessary for the hatching of salamander eggs.

Experiment I. Single egg cells of salamanders were tied loosely so that the nucleus was in one half of each cell. One sperm entered each half. The thread was tied tightly, separating the egg into two parts. Each part developed into an adult.

The following statements are based on Experiment I only. Use the same Key to classify them.

28. _B_ The egg nucleus is necessary for development.

29. _C_ The presence or absence of cytoplasm is of no importance.

30. _C_ The absence of a sperm nucleus makes development impossible.

31. _D_ The two halves of the tied egg developed into adults.

32. _A_ Only one nucleus is necessary for development to occur.

33. _C_ Each adult will be only half the size of a normal salamander.

Experiment II. *Unfertilized* frog eggs were divided into two groups. Group A was untreated. A needle was dipped into frog blood and was inserted into the eggs in Group B. Group B developed into adult frogs. The eggs in Group A soon died.

The next four items are based on the information from Experiments I and II. Use the same Key to classify each statement.

34. _B_ The sperm nucleus is necessary for development.

35. _B_ The absence of a sperm nucleus makes development impossible.

36. _C_ The presence or absence of cytoplasm is unimportant.

37. _A_ The absence of a sperm nucleus does not prevent development.

Experiment III. Salamander eggs were fertilized. The zygotes were cut in half, with one half containing the nucleus. The half with a nucleus developed into an adult; the other half died.

Use the same Key and the results from Experiments I, II, and III to classify the following five statements.

38. _B_ The cytoplasm alone can produce an embryo.

39. _A_ Some interaction between a nucleus and the cytoplasm is necessary for continued development of an embryo.

40. _B_ Cutting a cell into halves destroys its powers of development.

41. _A_ Eggs can develop without fertilization by sperm but not without a nucleus.

42. _C_ DNA diffuses into the cytoplasm from the nucleus to begin development.

The next eight items are based on the following graph. The graph shows the effects of temperature on the hatching time of insects.

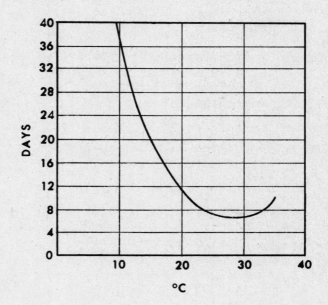

Use the following Key to classify the statements.

KEY A Supported by the data
    B Contradicted by the data
    C Neither supported nor contradicted by the data

43. _C_ The adult insect probably survives best at a temperature around 28°C.

44. _A_ The lowest temperature at which the insects will hatch is about 11°C.

45. _A_ The shortest time required for hatching is about seven days.

46. _B_ The time required for hatching decreases as the temperature rises from 28° to 34°C.

47. _B_ The rate of embryonic development increases with an increase in temperature above 25°C.

48. _A_ At 28°C, the insect has the fastest rate of embryonic development and the shortest time to hatching.

49. _C_ The insect eggs die at a temperature of 35°C.

50. _A_ The environmental temperature is critical to the rate of embryonic development of insects.

_____

Use the following information and Key to classify the next six hypotheses.

At a temperature of 30°C, fertilized frog eggs developed into tadpoles about twice as fast as did those kept at a temperature of 20°C.

KEY A Supported by experimental data
     B Contradicted by experimental data
     C Requires further experimentation

51. _C_ At a temperature of 60°C, frog eggs will grow into tadpoles four times as fast as at 20°C.

52. _B_ Frog eggs cannot hatch at temperatures below 25°C.

53. _C_ Salamander eggs develop twice as fast at 30°C as they do at 20°C.

54. _C_ Frog eggs develop abnormally at temperatures below 20°C.

55. _A_ Temperature affects the rate at which frog eggs develop into tadpoles.

56. _C_ In frog eggs, temperature and rate of development are directly proportional between 20° and 30°C.

_____

The next four items are based on the following diagrams of embryonic development.

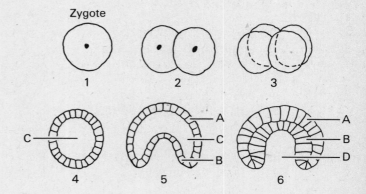

57. The cells of Layer A will give rise to which system?

*   A Nervous
     B Reproductive
     C Digestive
     D Circulatory

58. Which of the following occurs between Stages 1 and 2?

     A Fusion of egg and sperm
*   B Mitotic division
     C Reduction of chromosome number by one-half
     D Major differentiation

59. Between Stages 2 and 3,

     A the blastula forms.
     B gastrulation occurs.
*   C cleavage occurs.
     D the embryo increases in size.

60. Cavity D in Stage 6 will become

    A the spinal cord.
*   B the digestive system.
    C filled with tissue.
    D the body cavity.

_____

The next seven items are based on the following Key, which lists the three processes of development. Relate each phrase below with one of these processes.

KEY A Increase in cell number
      B Growth
      C Differentiation

61. _A_ Division of the zygote

62. _C_ Muscle cells, nerve cells, and skin cells

63. _C_ Formation of neural folds

64. _B_ A reason that food is necessary

65. _A_ Cancer

66. _C_ Development of the nervous system from the ectoderm

67. _B_ A change in size

_____

68. Primrose plants grown at $22^{\circ}C$ have red flowers. Those grown at temperatures above $30^{\circ}C$ have white flowers. This is a result of

    A a metabolic disfunction.
*   B environmental influence on gene expression.
    C abnormal induction and differentiation during development.
    D incomplete dominance.

9 Change Through Time—Evolution

INFORMATION AND DEFINITIONS

1. What did Lamarck and Darwin have in common? Both

    A originated the idea of evolution.
* B tried to explain how evolution occurs.
    C tried to explain mutation.
    D believed that organisms do not change.

2. If we were to assume that species do not change, we would expect to find

    A the simplest fossils in the oldest rocks.
    B the simplest fossils in the newest rocks.
* C the same kind of fossils in old and new rocks.
    D no fossils in any rocks.

3. Darwin based much of his theory of evolution on

* A the struggle for existence.
    B mistakes in DNA replication.
    C environmentally acquired characteristics.
    D the use and disuse of organs.

4. Darwin's idea of natural selection assumed

    A a stable, unchanging population of animals.
* B the survival value of random differences.
    C the inheritance of acquired characteristics.
    D that environmental stimuli caused changes in body structure.

5. Our present-day horse is much larger than its ancestors. Which statement below would help to explain this change based on Darwin's reasoning?

    A At some time in the past, a mutation occurred.
    B Early horses had to run fast to escape enemies. Thus they developed large muscles and long legs.
* C Large horses survived, small ones died, thus leaving only the large animals.
    D Early horses had to stretch for food on the trees. Thus they developed longer legs and necks.

6. The human embryo and embryos of all other animals with backbones have gill slits. This best supports the idea that

    A fish are our closest relatives.
    B the embryo breathes under water.
* C all animals with backbones are related.
    D fish are in the same species as humans.

7. Which of the following is *not* true of a theory?

    A It has stood the test of time.
* B It has been proven true.
    C It has been revised as new facts were found.
    D it has provided a basis for experimentation.

8. The use of bacteria in studies of natural selection and biological processes is

    A not possible because they cause diseases.
* B advantageous because large numbers are produced quickly.
    C limited; the information does not apply to other organisms.
    D not accepted as a valid experimental approach.

9. Humans have been able to get traits they want in organisms by

* A artificial selection.
    B random mating of organisms.
    C natural selection.
    D cloning of organisms.

10. Assume that a species lives in an area where there are many predators. Also assume that this species has no means of defense other than running. You would expect that

    A the species would develop long legs because of much use.
* B fewer short-legged individuals would survive than long-legged ones.
    C mutations would cause other methods of defense to develop.
    D the species would become extinct.

11. The characteristics of a species are determined by

* A the characteristics of the individual members of the species that survive and reproduce.
    B the amount of food and territory available to each member.
    C differential expression of a common genetic makeup.
    D divergent or convergent evolution of the species.

12. Which of the following ideas was *not* part of Darwin's hypothesis of natural selection?

    A Individual members of a species are different from each other.
    B The size of a population increases because of reproduction.
    C Growth of a population cannot continue indefinitely.
* D Each parent contributes one-half of its genes to its offspring through the sperm or the egg.

13. In humans, the appendix is an example of

* A a vestigial organ.
    B homology.
    C natural selection.
    D a mutation.

14. Two closely related species that have very different characteristics are the result of

    A convergence.
    B homology.
    C predation.
* D divergence.

_____

For the next ten items, use the following Key to identify each statement.

KEY This statement is consistent with the views of

    A Lamarck, but not Darwin.
    B Darwin, but not Lamarck.
    C both Lamarck and Darwin.
    D neither Lamarck nor Darwin.

15. __B__ The environment can select for flies resistant to DDT.

16. __C__ Fly populations can develop a resistance to DDT.

17. _A_ DDT can cause flies to become resistant.

18. _B_ In a dry climate, organisms with heavy skin survive and leave more offspring.

19. _C_ The environment is an important factor in the evolution of organisms.

20. _A_ Variety in living things can be explained by adjustments of an individual to a certain way of life.

21. _C_ Populations of organisms are limited by a struggle for existence.

22. _A_ Because early horses had to run fast to escape their enemies, they developed large muscles and long legs.

23. _B_ Larger horses survived, smaller ones died, thus leaving only populations of large horses.

24. _A_ Early giraffes had to stretch for food on the trees, thus developing long legs and necks.

APPLICATION AND INQUIRY

Use the Key to identify the relationship between the pairs of statements in each of the next five items.

KEY A _1_ (observational) is explained by _2_ (theoretical).
  B _1_ (theoretical) explains _2_ (observational).
  C Both are observational.
  D Both are theoretical.

25. _B_ _1._ Birds and mammals evolved from reptiles thousands of years ago. _2._ Birds, mammals, and reptiles have many anatomical similarities.

26. _A_ _1._ Organisms living today differ from fossil forms. _2._ The forms living today have evolved from a common ancestor.

27. _D_ _1._ Modern organisms are the result of change through time. _2._ In general, organisms have evolved from simple to complex.

28. _C_ _1._ Animals belonging to the same species look alike. _2._ Animals belonging to the same species can mate and produce fertile offspring.

29. _A_ _1._ The great Dane and the poodle belong to the species _Canis familiaris_, while the wolf belongs to the species _Canis lupus._ _2._ The poodle and the great Dane have a more recent common ancestor than the great Dane and the wolf.

30. What is the most impressive evidence for the idea that organisms have evolved?

* A Fossil records
  B Family trees
  C Studies of modern organisms
  D Published works of authorities

The next four items are based on the following experiments.

Experiment 1. A barn was sprayed with the insecticide DDT for two years. Flies were killed throughout both years. After three years of spraying, however, flies were present in the barn even on the day after spraying.

Experiment 2. After the third year, flies from the barn were captured and grown in a laboratory for ten generations. The tenth generation of flies was tested and found to be resistant to DDT.

A second colony of flies from an unsprayed barn also was grown for ten generations in the laboratory. These flies could be killed by DDT.

31. The major problem under investigation in these experiments was

    A how does DDT kill a fly?
    B how can the fly population be reduced by using DDT.
    C how do flies reproduce in a barn?
*   D how do fly populations that are resistant to DDT originate?

32. The resistance level that developed in the fly population

    A was caused by the DDT.
    B was a result of immigration of flies from unsprayed areas.
    C can be explained by the effects of DDT on the breathing mechanisms of flies.
*   D would occur rarely in individual flies regardless of the presence or absence of DDT.

33. In the barn, the DDT seemed to act as a

    A developmental factor.
    B growth factor.
    C nutrient factor.
*   D selective factor.

34. Which result of these experiments showed that resistance to DDT is inherited?

    A DDT-resistant flies were present in the barn.
*   B DDT resistance continued through ten generations in the absence of DDT.
    C No resistant flies were present after ten generations when the parent flies were not resistant.
    D DDT killed flies when first used in the barn.

35. Which of the following was *not* explained by Darwin's theory of natural selection?

    A Adaptation
    B Fossils
*   C Sources of variability in species
    D Differences in species in similar environments on different continents

36. "Natural selection may result in the formation of new species." This statement

*   A is a hypothesis.
    B represents data.
    C is a fact.
    D contains an experimental design.

37. Which of the following illustrates Darwin's theory of evolution?

    A People who get a good body tan have children with a slight tan.

    B If a mother plays a piano during pregnancy, she will have a musically gifted child.

    C Birds do not eat viceroy butterflies because they resembly monarch butterflies.

*   D Breeding greyhounds for speed changes their inheritance.

38. The ptarmigan is an arctic bird. In winter its feathers are white; in summer they are brown. Which is the most reasonable explanation of how this color change has developed?

*   A A series of mutations over a long period of time had selective value.

    B Continued exposure to long periods of cold caused the change.

    C The different types of food available in summer and in winter caused the change.

    D The color changes to protect the bird from predators.

39. Of 357 similar weeds germinating in a 2 m by 3 m area, only 62 reached maturity. Which of the following aspects of Darwin's theory of natural selection best explains this observation?

    A All members of a species vary in their traits.

    B Many variations of a species are inherited.

*   C A struggle for existence occurs among members of a species.

    D Offspring inherit variations, and great differences arise.

Use the Key to identify the next five statements.

KEY A Observation
       B Hypothesis
       C Prediction

40. A On the voyage of the *Beagle*, Darwin noted that ". . . in the Pampean formation great fossil animals were covered with armour like that on the existing armadillos . . . ."

41. B This is an idea that has served to explain or to account for the known data.

42. B Species, contrary to almost universal belief, are not unchanging but actually do change over long periods of time.

43. C In Alabama, there is a strip of land where the soil is almost black. In other parts of the state, the soil is red. The lizards living in the area of dark soil should be darker than in other parts of the state.

44. A The early stages of bird and pig embryos look very similar.

The next four items are based on the following information and graph.

A tropical island was heavily infested with mosquitoes. It was sprayed with DDT over a period of several months. Daily counts of population size yielded the following data.

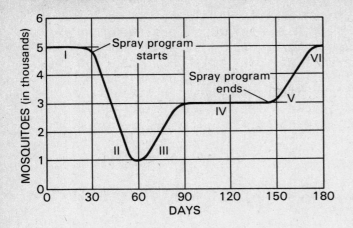

45. A change in the genetic makeup of a population as a result of natural selection is illustrated best by the section of the graph labeled

- A   I.
- B   II.
- *   C   III.
- D   IV.

46. On the basis of this graph, which of the following statements can be made?

- A   Mosquitoes are not sensitive to DDT.
- *   B   The population decreases after spraying.
- C   The population is permanently reduced in 120 days after spraying.
- D   All of the original mosquitoes were killed by the end of 30 days.

47. The difference in the genetic makeup of the mosquitoes is the greatest between Points

- A   I and IV.
- *   B   I and VI.
- C   III and IV.
- D   IV and VI.

48. The number of mosquitoes being born and the number dying are balanced in the section of the graph labeled

- A   II.
- B   III.
- *   C   IV.
- D   V.

49. Sexual reproduction is a significant factor in evolution. This is true because it provides for

- A   the production of genes.
- B   the only means for continuing any species.
- *   C   great variation in offspring.
- D   changes in how DNA duplicates itself.

50. We could say that evolution is a process

- A   that occurs rapidly.
- B   in which the environment acts on genes to change the makeup of the organism.
- *   C   that is conservative and remodels existing structures.
- D   whereby organs become vestigial when the animal does not use them.

The next six items are concerned with interpretation of the fossil data in the table. Use these data and the Key to classify the hypotheses.

DISTRIBUTION OF MAMMALS

MILLIONS OF YEARS AGO	NORTH AMERICA	SOUTH AMERICA	BOTH
1	22 kinds	22 kinds	22 kinds
12	25 kinds	27 kinds	2 kinds

KEY   The hypothesis is

A   contrary to the data.
B   contrary to the evolution theory.
C   logical on the basis of the data and evolution theory.
D   logical on the basis of evolution theory but not related to the data.

51. __C__ At some time between 12 million and 1 million years ago, a land bridge appeared between North and South America.

52. __A__ Some kinds of mammals were present 1 million years ago in North America that were not present in South America, and vice versa.

53. __B__ Twenty-two kinds of mammals were common to both regions in the period 1 million years ago. This might be explained by similar evolution taking place at the same time on both continents.

54. __A__ Mammals were rare in the period 12 millions years ago.

55. __C__ Sometime between 1 and 12 million years ago, many mammals migrated to the north and to the south.

56. __D__ Mammals replaced reptiles as the dominant vertebrates in North and South America.

_____

The next seven items are based on the following diagram. The diagram shows sedimentary rock layers and certain organisms found in them. The layers in Locality I were found several kilometers away from those in Locality II. The labels a-d and 1-4 refer to the different strata.

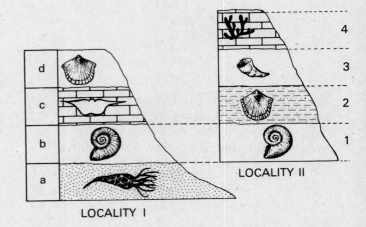

LOCALITY I

57. What is the evidence that these are sedimentary rocks?

   A   The fossils
   B   The layers
* C   Both of these
   D   Neither of these

58. The increase in complexity in organisms through time

   A   is clearly shown here.
   B   is indicated by their positions in the rock strata.
* C   cannot be inferred from this diagram.
   D   is not possible.

59. Assume that no geological shifts have taken place. If this is the case, the organisms in

   A   Stratum a are the simplest.
   B   Stratum d are the simplest.
* C   Stratum a are the oldest.
   D   Stratum d are the oldest.

66

60. Which stratum in Locality II might be continuous with Stratum d in Locality I?

* A Stratum 2
  B Stratum 3
  C Stratum 4
  D None of the strata

61. Which of the following can be inferred from the study of the fossils in the various strata in the diagram?

  A Organisms have changed through time.
  B Organisms change structurally from simple to complex.
* C The relative geologic ages of two specific fossils can be determined.
  D The organisms in the diagram are the only ones that were living in the areas when the fossils were formed.

62. The reason Stratum c does not occur in Locality II may be because

  A there is no record of volcanic activity in Locality II.
* B Erosion may have washed away Stratum c.
  C It is actually above those shown here.
  D It is in Stratum 4 of Locality II but is not shown.

63. Assume that there has been no disturbance of the strata. We would expect to find the organisms in Locality II, Stratum 3, also in Locality I,

  A Stratum d.
* B the stratum just above Stratum d.
  C Stratum c.
  D the stratum just below Stratum a.

10 Evolution at Work

INFORMATION AND DEFINITIONS

1. Mutation is a basic source of new kinds of genes in a species. Variability is increased greatly by

*   A recombination of genes.
    B asexual reproduction.
    C natural selection.
    D divergent evolution.

2. A plant has an allele that gives it a survival advantage. Over time, the percentage of this allele in the population has increased. This probably is due to

    A a need of the plant.
    B mutation.
*   C natural selection.
    D artificial selection.

3. A flower grower discovered a mutant plant and decided to cross-breed it to obtain a new variety. This is an example of

    A a chance mutation and natural selection.
    B an induced mutation and natural selection.
    C an induced mutation and artificial selection.
*   D a chance mutation and artificial selection.

4. From the point of view of evolution, the greatest advantage of sexual reproduction is the

*   A variety of organisms it can produce.
    B consistency of traits that appear in each generation.
    C continuance of the species.
    D fact that fewer eggs are fertilized.

5. Evolution takes place more rapidly among organisms that reproduce sexually than among those that reproduce asexually. This is true because

    A sexual reproduction is more hazardous than asexual, and only the fit survive.
    B asexual reproduction occurs only in one-celled organisms.
*   C sexual reproduction is more likely to produce a variety of offspring.
    D sexual reproduction is slower than asexual reproduction in producing offspring.

6. Assume that, in the gene pool of a human population, 62 percent of the reproductive cells carry the dominant A allele. The percentage of reproductive cells carrying a alleles would be

    A 62%.
    B 76%.
*   C 38%.
    D 100%.

7. Heredity of flower color in a certain plant is determined by one pair of alleles. The gene for red flowers R is dominant to the gene for white flowers r. We can determine the gene frequency in the plant population by knowing *only* the

    A number of individuals in the population.
    B percentage of individuals in the population.
*   C percentage of white flowers in the sample.
    D number of red flowers in the sample.

8. A new species of organism is formed when

    A a series of mutations makes an individual phenotypically different from others in the population.
    B an individual is isolated from the rest of the species by a geographic barrier.
    C the climate of a population changes drastically.
*   D a group of organisms no longer can interbreed with other closely related species.

9. Why are many types of animals found *only* on the continent of Australia?

    A the climate is more suitable for these animals.
*   B It is geographically isolated from other continents.
    C There are no native predators.
    D There is less climatic variation than on other continents.

10. Which best describes the theory of evolution?

*   A Living species of today are descendants of species in past ages.
    B Changes in an individual are brought about by influences in its environment.
    C Mutations cause hereditary variations.
    D Change seldom occurs in an evolutionary event.

11. Sickle cell heterozygotes are

    A susceptible to malaria.
*   B resistant to malaria.
    C incapable of passing the sickle cell trait to their offspring.
    D affected by the sickle cell trait more severely than homozygotes.

12. Patterns of heredity in a population are the direct result of the

*   A gene frequencies.
    B environmental influences.
    C recessive genes.
    D mutations.

13. In the DNA segment A-T-G-C-A-T, what kind of mutation would produce a new segment A-A-G-C-A-T?

    A Insertion
    B Deletion
*   C Substitution
    D Recessive

14. Which of the following is *not* influenced by mutation?

*   A Emigration
    B Natural selection
    C Evolution
    D Gene frequency

15. A substance is termed mutagenic if it

    A decreases mutation rate.
*   B increases mutation rate.
    C produces genetic isolation.
    D causes gene frequencies to remain stable.

16. The Hardy-Weinberg principle does *not* operate when

    A gene frequencies are the same in males and females.
    B a population breeds at random.
    C the population is very large.
*   D one allele of a gene pair mutates more frequently than the other.

17. Which of the following is *not* necessary for evolution to occur?

*   A Polyploidy
    B Genetic variability
    C Natural selection
    D Reproductive isolation

The next three items are based on data about peppered moths.

A large number of moths were captured and marked for identification. Then, 488 dark and 496 light moths were released. Later, 34 dark and 62 light moths were recaptured.

18. Which of the following would be the most reasonable assumption?

    A The moths were released in a forest with dark tree trunks.
    B Identical numbers of moths must be released.
*   C The moths were released in a forest that had many light tree trunks.
    D Not enough moths were recaptured to permit a conclusion.

19. The moths were marked with paint on the *under* side. They were marked in this way because

    A it would be easier to identify recaptured moths.
    B it was easier to mark them in this way.
*   C paint on the upper side might have introduced another variable.
    D paint will wear off the upper side more rapidly.

20. This experiment on moth populations provides data on

*   A the effect of environment on the survival of favorable variations.
    B reproduction as a factor in maintaining populations.
    C the survival rate of moths in a forest environment.
    D the ability of a species to exist in an unnatural environment.

The next 11 items refer to the following information about the Galapagos finches.

The island finches are almost identical, except that birds on different islands have different beaks. Some of the finches have woodpecker-like beaks, and others have beaks like sparrows. Some have parrot-like beaks, and others have insect-catching beaks. All of these finches have very short flying ranges, and none of them migrate.

Use this Key to evaluate the next statements.

KEY A Agrees with evolution theory; is supported by the data
      B Agrees with evolution theory; is *not* supported by the data
      C Does not agree with evolution theory; data show it is false
      D Does not agree with evolution theory; data do *not* show it is false

21. A The different species of finches probably originated from a common ancestor.

22. D If fossil records were available, they would show no evidence of the evolution of these birds.

23. C Different finch species compete for the same food.

24. A Beak differentiation is one basis for considering the finches as separate species.

25. B Fossils of finches in lower strata of the islands are more alike than the present-day finches on these islands.

26. _A_ The gene pools on the various islands were separated originally by a geographic barrier.

27. _A_ The various adaptations of these finches improve their chances of survival.

28. _A_ The genes in the population of the parrot-finch species are different from those of the woodpecker-finch species.

29. _A_ The ancestor of the finches had some favorable variations that permitted diversity in the later species.

30. _C_ The birds have become less diversified over the years because they interbreed.

31. _A_ The finches are adapted to a variety of environments.

_____

For the next four items, select from the Key the aspect of Darwin's theory of natural selection that is supported by the observation.

KEY A Individuals of a species vary in their traits.
    B There is a struggle for existence among individuals of a species.
    C Favorable variations are passed on to offspring and in time great differences arise.

32. _A_ Beetles from three islands will interbreed. The island groups have characteristics as follows: Island A -- 6 black stripes on a green body; Island B -- 4 black stripes on a green body; Island C -- solid green body.

33. _A_ A cross between a terrier and a poodle produces fertile offspring called terripoos.

34. _C_ Strains of wheat that have high yields and insect resistance have been developed from less desirable strains.

35. _C_ Squirrels on the North Rim of the Grand Canyon differ in many respects from those on the South Rim. (The river and canyon prevent passage from one side to the other).

_____

36. If a mutant allele gives an organism a slight advantage, what will happen to the allele?

   A Since it is a mutation, it will soon be dropped from the gene pool.
* B It will remain in the gene pool and have a selective advantage.
   C Dominant genes will mask it, so its effect will not be noted.
   D The mutants will come to be considered a different species after ten generations.

_____

The next three items are based on the following diagram of four populations. These populations interbreed as shown by the overlapping circles.

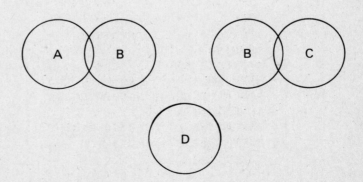

37. How many species are shown?

     A 1
*   B 2
     C 3
     D 4

38. How many species would there be if Population A disappeared?

     A 1
*   B 2
     C 3
     D 4

39. How many species would there be if Population B disappeared?

     A 1
     B 2
*   C 3
     D 4

---

40. A geographic area has a large pheasant population. This fact probably indicates that

     A the average age of pheasants in the population has increased considerably.
     B the pheasants reproduce slowly.
     C the ratio of predators to pheasants is higher than normal.
*   D pheasants are well adapted to this area.

41. Harmful recessive genes remain in a population of organisms because they

     A are retained for future survival value.
     B are controlled by the Hardy-Weinberg Law.
*   C are carried by heterozygous individuals.
     D cannot be eliminated except by increase in mutation rate.

42. Since environments change over long periods of time, what must happen to populations of organisms if they are to survive?

     A New species must frequently be created.
     B The reproductive rate must increase.
     C Such populations must interbreed with other populations to survive.
*   D Members of the population must differ from one another for natural selection to operate.

43. Although Madagascar is separated from Africa only by a narrow strait, many plants and animals common on the mainland are unknown on the island. This fact illustrates the principle of

     A incomplete dominance.
     B immigration and emigration.
*   C reproductive isolation.
     D Hardy-Weinberg.

The next five items are based on the following data and Key.

A biologist observed two groups of salamanders. The biologist noted that the two groups

KEY A had different colorations and arrangements of spots.
       B had a common ancestor, as shown by the fossil record.
       C lived in different isolated habitats.
       D could interbreed and produce fertile offspring.

44. <u>D</u> Which is the best evidence that the salamanders are all of one species?

45. <u>C</u> Which suggests that they existed in a condition that favored the evolution of separate species?

46. __D__ A change in which observed condition would eventually produce two separate species?

47. __B__ Which observation includes an interpretation of data?

48. __A__ Which condition could be changed by selective breeding?

_____

The next four items are based on the following data on Rh factor in the blood of a particular population. The presence of Rh antigen is dominant. Individuals who do not have Rh antigens have a homozygous recessive genotype.

	Rh POSITIVE	Rh NEGATIVE
NUMBER	1,008	192
PERCENTAGE	84%	16%

49. The frequency of the recessive gene in the population is

* A 0.4.
  B 0.6.
  C 0.16.
  D 0.84.

50. The frequency of the dominant gene in the population is

  A 0.4.
* B 0.6.
  C 0.16.
  D 0.84.

51. What proportion of this population would be heterozygous for Rh factor?

  A 0.36
  B 0.16
  C 0.84
* D 0.48

52. If this population were to continue to mate randomly, what proportion of the next generation would be expected to be homozygous for Rh factor?

* A 0.36
  B 0.16
  C 0.84
  D 0.48

73

11 Human Evolution

1. The brain size of human fossil skulls indicates that through millions of years the size

    A reached a peak.
    B has remained constant.
*   C has increased.
    D has been decreasing.

2. The history of ancient people has been difficult to determine from fossils because

    A too much limestone has replaced bone.
*   B fossil evidence is not complete.
    C no good method of dating fossils has been found.
    D there is no organized way to identify human fossils.

3. The fossil record indicates that

    A the ancestors of humans were apes.
    B people have never been any different than they are today.
*   C humans and apes have evolved along separate lines for a long time.
    D people originally evolved in North America.

4. All members of the species *Homo sapiens* are grouped together because they

    A are similar in appearance.
    B have only slightly different skull shapes.
    C have only slightly different distribution of body hair.
*   D can interbreed and produce fertile offspring.

5. With fossil skulls alone, scientists can determine

    A hair color.
    B culture.
    C texture of skin.
*   D facial features.

6. The names given to prehistoric humans generally refer to their

    A skull size.
    B forehead shape.
*   C location.
    D discoverer.

7. The fossil primate that is thought to have been on the same evolutionary line as modern humans is

    A *Homo erectus.*
    B Neanderthal.
*   C *Australopithecus.*
    D Cro-Magnon.

8. Bones of a wooly mammoth are found with those of a human. The person most likely was

*   A Cro-Magnon.
    B *Homo sapiens.*
    C Neanderthal.
    D *Homo erectus.*

9. People try to select and breed plants and animals for certain desirable traits. This artificial selection usually works against

    A humans, because mutations produce poor offspring.
*   B natural selection of traits.
    C development of desired characteristics.
    D continuation of the organism.

10. Artificial breeding of animals for domestication probably was accomplished by

    A breeding wild and tame animals to produce heterozygotes.
    B taming adult wild animals and then breeding them.
*   C selecting the tamest animals for breeding.
    D capturing animals in pens and allowing them to breed.

11. One of the earliest examples of artificial breeding is the development of

*   A grains that were suitable for cultivation.
    B breeds of dogs to aid in hunting.
    C horses that could run swiftly.
    D strains of fish with high protein content.

12. Probably the first people to live in permanent villages were

    A hunters.
    B farmers.
*   C fishers.
    D herders.

13. People could live in permanent villages only after they could be sure of

    A a constant climate.
*   B continued food supply.
    C protection against invaders.
    D good soil to grow crops.

14. Which illustrates best an accomplishment of humans that other animals could not achieve?

    A Organized labor systems
    B Family unity and care
*   C Passing on written knowledge
    D Ability to learn

APPLICATION AND INQUIRY

The next four items are based on the following data from studies of four skeletons from different excavations in the same general region of Africa.

NUMBER	BRAIN SIZE (ml)	LENGTH OF ARMS AND LEGS	ITEMS WITH SKELETON
1	400	Arms longer than legs	None
2	1300	Arms shorter than legs	Metal arrow
3	600	Arms same length as legs	None
4	1000	Arms shorter than legs	Stone ax

15. The skeleton most like that of modern humans is

    A 1.
*   B 2.
    C 3.
    D 4.

16. The presence of an arrowhead near Skeleton 2 indicates that the individual most likely

    A was killed by an arrow.
    B used fire for cooking.
    C had domesticated wild animals.
*   D lived at a time when tools were used.

17. The individuals that walked the most nearly erect probably were

    A 1 and 2.
    B 1 and 3.
    C 1 and 4.
*   D 2 and 4.

18. If we assume that the four skeletons are on the same evolutionary line, the most probable order (from oldest to most recent) is

    A 2, 4, 3, 1.
    B 1, 4, 3, 2.
*   C 1, 3, 4, 2.
    D 2, 3, 4, 1.

---

19. South American Indians characteristically have Type-O blood. If a group of South American Indians were found that had Type A as well as Type O, it is most likely that

    A intermarriage within Indian families had taken place.
    B many new mutations had taken place.
*   C genes from another group of humans had been introduced.
    D a change in the environment had occurred.

20. Cro-Magnon people are placed in the same species as modern people. To be sure that this grouping fits our definition of species, we would have to observe Cro-Magnon's

    A social patterns and use of tools.
*   B ability to breed with modern humans and produce fertile offspring.
    C ability to integrate into modern society.
    D anatomy and physiology as well as chromosome number.

The next eight items are based on the maps on page 77. These maps show the distribution of Species X on two continents -- Eurasia and North America.

The shaded areas are the present ranges of Species X. The outlined areas are previous ranges. The number in each outlined range indicates how many millions of years ago Species X occupied the area.

I, II, III, and IV are living populations of Species X.

21. Where did the species probably originate?

*   A Eurasia
    B Eastern North America
    C Western North America
    D Both continents at about the same time

22. The most likely migration route of Species X was from

    A north to south in Eurasia.
    B east to west in North America
    C east to west in Eurasia.
*   D western Eurasia to North America.

23. Which two populations are the most similar genetically?

    A I and II
    B I and IV
    C II and III
*   D III and IV

24. The data indicate that the area occupied by this species has

    A continued to increase.
    B continued to decrease.
*   C increased and then decreased.
    D decreased and then increased.

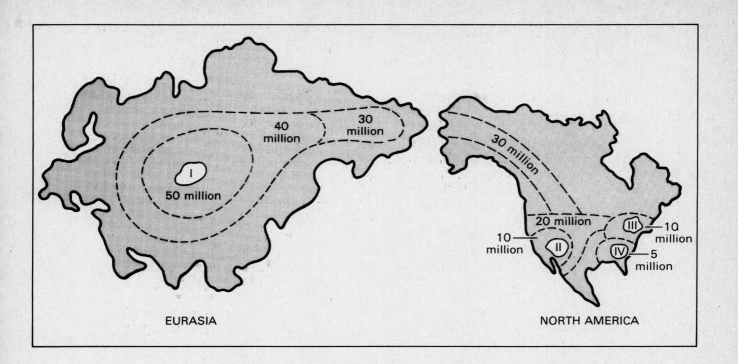

EURASIA

NORTH AMERICA

25. Which is the oldest population?

*　A　I
　　B　II
　　C　III
　　D　IV

26. How many populations probably existed 10 million years ago?

　　A　1
　　B　2
*　C　3
　　D　4

27. How many populations probably existed 50 million years ago?

*　A　1
　　B　2
　　C　3
　　D　4

28. Which living population is least likely to be able to interbreed with the other three?

*　A　I
　　B　II
　　C　III
　　D　IV

Use this Key to classify each of the next seven items.

KEY　A　Problem
　　　B　Observation
　　　C　Hypothesis or theory

29. __B__ The races of humans have many traits in common.

30. __C__ Of the different races, Caucasians are most heterozygous.

31. __C__ Humans are more closely related to the apes than to any other animal group.

32. __A__ How did the various races of humans originate?

33. __C__ All humans have a common ancestry.

34. __B__ Racial differences are composites of many phenotypic characteristics.

35. __B__ Interracial marriages produce fertile offspring.

For the next 19 items, use the following Key. Classify the human characteristics according to their biological survival value in an ancient natural environment.

KEY A Physical advantage of humans
    B Cultural or behavioral advantage of humans
    C Disadvantage of humans
    D Neither an advantage nor a disadvantage

36. _A_ Upright posture

37. _A_ Highly developed eyes

38. _D_ A distinct chin

39. _C_ Poorly developed organs of smell

40. _A_ Opposable thumb

41. _B_ Ability to make tools

42. _B_ Formation of groups of for hunting.

43. _A_ Long life span

44. _A_ Long legs

45. _B_ Development of villages

46. _A_ Large brain

47. _B_ Development of language

48. _D_ Small teeth

49. _B_ Domestication of plants and animals

50. _B_ Ability to eat almost anything

51. _A_ Straight leg bones

52. _C_ High energy requirement

53. _D_ Development of religious rituals

54. _B_ Verbal transmission of experience from one generation to the next

---

12   Diversity in the Living World

INFORMATION AND DEFINITIONS

1. According to the system of binomial nomenclature, the organism *Acetabularia mediterranea* is most closely related to

    A *Mediterranea crassa.*
    B *Mediterranea crenulata.*
*   C *Acetabularia crenulata.*
    D *Crenulata acetabularia.*

2. A family includes closely related

    A orders.
    B classes.
*   C genera.
    D phyla.

3. Which of these categories contains the greatest number of different kinds of organisms?

    A Genus
    B Family
*   C Phylum
    D Class

4. In which of these categories are the organisms most closely related?

    A Family
    B Class
    C Order
*   D Genus

5. Examples of homologous structures are

    A tentacle of jellyfish and rays of starfish.
*   B wings of birds and forelegs of cows.
    C lungs of humans and gills of fishes.
    D cilia of paramecia and hair of mammals.

6. *Felix tigris* is an example of binomial nomenclature. These two words include

    A order and family.
    B phyla and species.
    C order and genus.
*   D genus and species.

7. In which of the following categories would the largest number of the following specimens be placed: lion, seal, whale, human, bird, snail, earthworm?

*   A Kingdom
    B Species
    C Phylun
    D Order

8. Annelids are considered to be more advanced than Coelenterates. This is because they have

    A flattened bodies and two main layers of cells.
*   B segmented bodies with a circulatory system.
    C two main layers of cells and their bodies are covered by a shell.
    D radial symmetry and "stinging cells."

9. Plant Species A flowers during long periods of daylight. Species B flowers only during short periods of daylight. Species A and B were raised in the laboratory under different light conditions. They cross-fertilized and produced seeds that would grow. What is the best reason for considering them separate species?

*   A They cannot interbreed in nature.
    B They have different light requirements.
    C They are structurally different.
    D They do not occur together in nature.

APPLICATION AND INQUIRY

The next three items are based on the following diagram of a sea squirt.

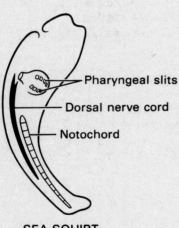

Pharyngeal slits
Dorsal nerve cord
Notochord

SEA SQUIRT
Immature Stage
(free-swimming)

SEA SQUIRT
Adult Stage
(attached)

10. The sea squirt belongs in which phylum?

*   A Chordata
    B Porifera
    C Vertebrata
    D Coelenterata

11. Sea squirts are grouped in the same phylum as

    A oysters, squids, and clams.
*   B dogs, fish, and people.
    C crayfish, spiders, and scorpions.
    D starfish, sea cucumbers, and sea urchins.

12. All members of the phylum to which the sea squirt belongs have three things in common. At some time in their lives, they have pharyngeal slits, a hollow dorsal nerve cord, and

    A a dorsal heart.
    B lateral scales.
*   C a notochord.
    D posterior sense organs.

From each of the following groups of animals, select the one animal that is *least* like the other three. Base your selections on our present system of classification.

13. A Bat
    B Bluejay
    C Flying squirrel
  * D Honeybee

14. A Grasshopper
    B Mosquito
  * C Spider
    D Butterfly

15. A Snake
    B Lizard
  * C Frog
    D Alligator

16. *A Earthworm
    B Millipede
    C Crab
    D Centipede

17. A Catfish
    B Bass
    C Mackerel
  * D Whale

18. *A Starfish
    B Oyster
    C Octopus
    D Snail

19. A Centipede
  * B Octopus
    C Crayfish
    D Spider

20. A Barn swallow
  * B Bat
    C Eagle
    D Penguin

21. A Dog
    B Cat
    C Seal
  * D Flying fish

22. A Sponge
    B Coral
    C Hydra
  * D Insect
    _____

The next five items are based on the following diagram and Key. Use the Key to classify the statements.

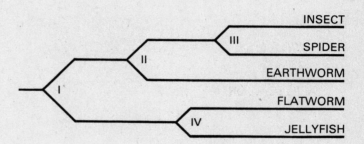

At which fork in the diagram were the contrasting characteristics listed below used to separate the organisms?

KEY A Fork I
    B Fork II
    C Fork III
    D Fork IV

23. _B_ External skeleton versus no skeleton

24. _A_ Segmentation versus no segmentation

25. _A_ Single body opening versus two body openings

26. _C_ Six legs versus eight legs

27. _B_ Jointed appendages versus no jointed appendages
    _____

The next three items are based on the classification of these animals.

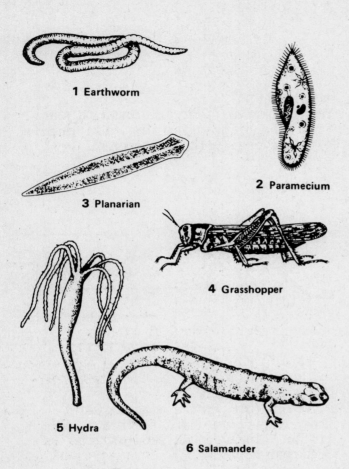

1 Earthworm

2 Paramecium

3 Planarian

4 Grasshopper

5 Hydra

6 Salamander

28. Suppose that 1, 2, 3, and 5 are placed in one group, and 4 and 6 in another. The respiratory feature on which the classification is based most likely is

    A tracheal tubes versus lungs.
    B moist versus dry respiratory surfaces.
    C control of respiration by nervous system versus *not* by nervous system.
*   D diffusion through body wall versus special respiratory organs.

29. Suppose 1, 4, and 6 are placed in one group, and 2, 3, and 5 are placed in another. The basis of this classification most likely is

*   A segmentation versus no segmentation.
    B backbone versus no backbone.
    C lungs versus no lungs.
    D separate sexes versus hermaphrodism.

30. Which of these organisms has an endoskeleton?

    A 1
    B 3
    C 4
*   D 6

_____

The next four items are based on the following description.

An aquatic organism has a smooth, slimy, gray-brown body. It is 30 cm long. It has a powerful, flat tail and a short, flat head with red external gills.

    This organism has four weak legs with toes but no toenails. It has a dorsal nerve cord, a skull, and a backbone. Early in its development, it has a notochord.

    The organism eats crayfish, fish eggs, and other water animals.

31. A clue to this organism's phylum is its

*   A notochord.
    B gray-brown color.
    C slimy body.
    D external gills.

32. This organism would be related most closely to a

    A millipede.
*   B fish.
    C shrimp.
    D spider.

33. This organism most likely is a(n)

    A fish.
    B reptile.
*   C amphibian.
    D arthropod.

34. What information above would be *least* valuable in classifying the organism? The aquatic organism

*   A was 30 cm long.
    B had a dorsal nerve cord.
    C had four weak legs.
    D had a notochord.

The next five items refer to the animals pictured below.

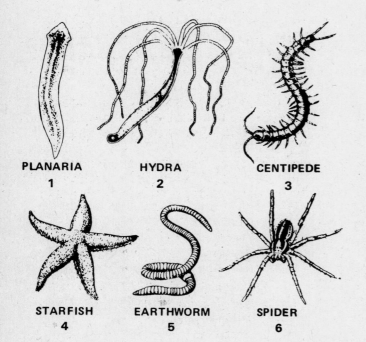

PLANARIA 1   HYDRA 2   CENTIPEDE 3

STARFISH 4   EARTHWORM 5   SPIDER 6

35. 1, 2, and 4 can be classified differently from the others on the basis of having

*   A no segmentation.
    B external skeletons.
    C radial symmetry.
    D jointed appendages.

36. Which of the organisms usually is placed in a phylum that contains mostly parasitic species?

*   A 1
    B 2
    C 4
    D 6

37. Organisms 3 and 6 can be classified differently from the others on the basis of the

    A presence of blood.
    B number of body layers.
    C presence of a nervous system.
*   D presence of jointed appendages.

38. Which of the following pairs represents organisms that usually are placed in the same phylum?

    A 1 and 2
    B 2 and 5
    C 3 and 5
*   D 3 and 6

39. Which of the organisms have digestive systems with only one opening?

*   A 1 and 2
    B 1 and 5
    C 2 and 3
    D 2 and 5

For the next six items, refer to the following table. (Fill in the blank spaces before answering the questions.)

	ORGANISM I	ORGANISM II	ORGANISM III	ORGANISM IV
PHYLUM	Arthropoda			
CLASS	Insecta			
ORDER	Lepidoptera	Lepidoptera		
FAMILY	Tortricidae	Psychidae		Tortricidae
GENUS	*Archips*	*Solenobia*	*Archips*	*Eulia*
SPECIES	*rosano*	*walshella*	*fervidona*	*pinatubana*

40. Which two organisms are related most closely?

    A I and II
*   B I and III
    C I and IV
    D II and IV

41. Which organism is the most *distantly* related to Organism IV?

    A I
*   B II
    C III
    D All are equally related.

42. Which organisms belong to the phylum Arthropoda?

    A I only
    B I and II only
    C I, II, and IV only
*   D All of them

43. Which organisms belong to the class Insecta?

    A I only
    B I, II, and IV only
    C I and IV only
*   D All of them

44. Which organisms belong to the same family?

    A I and III only
    B I and IV only
    C III and IV only
*   D I, III, and IV

45. Which of these organisms would have an internal skeleton?

    A II, III, and IV
    B All of them
*   C None of them
    D Insufficient information given to answer this

_____

The next four items are based on the following information.

In a group of ten organisms there are four obvious characteristics:

1.   All ten have teeth adapted for chewing.
2.   All ten have four legs.
3.   Eight have long snouts.
4.   Five have retractable claws.

84

46. The characteristic that most likely would group all the organisms in one category is

* A 1.
  B 2.
  C 3.
  D 4.

47. The characteristic that would be of the *least* help in classifying these organisms is

  A 1.
* B 2.
  C 3.
  D 4.

48. The group that may be most closely related is

  A 1.
  B 2.
  C 3.
* D 4.

49. Assume that we have determined that all the organisms with Characteristic 3 are closely related. Then,

* A all the organisms with Characteristic 4 are even more closely related.
  B they are all related to those with Characteristic 1.
  C they are more closely related to those with Characteristic 2 than to those with Characteristic 1.
  D three of those with long snouts have no claws.

---

50. Suppose breeding two kinds of animals always results in sterile offspring. The two kinds most likely are of the same

  A genus and the same species.
* B genus but different species.
  C species and same family.
  D species but different genera.

51. The formation of coacervates provides a clue to explain how

  A blue-green algae may have been the first organisms.
  B living things could have produced organic compounds.
  C protozoa obtain organic materials from the environment.
* D organic compounds, dissolved in the sea, might have formed primitive cells.

52. Assuming that all present-day Coelenterates are equally ancient, which group probably would have left the most complete fossil record?

* A Corals
  B Jellyfish
  C Hydra
  D Sea anemones

53. There are deposits of coal in Greenland and Antarctica. This indicates that

  A the earth is warmer today than it was when coal was deposited.
  B the plant species now found on these continents also lived during the Carboniferous period.
* C these areas were once warmer than they are at present.
  D in the past less light was available in these areas.

54. Which of the following would have been absent from the early atmosphere of the earth?

* A O_2
  B NH_3
  C CH_4
  D H_2O

55. Which is the most logical sequence for the appearance of molecules under conditions that probably existed on the early earth?

* A Ammonia - amino acids - proteins
  B Starch - glycogen - glucose
  C Glucose - glycogen - starch
  D Fats - carbohydrates - proteins

_____

For the next six items, determine the relationship between the pairs of statements. Use the Key to identify the relationships.

KEY The likelihood of

A 1 is greater than 2.
B 2 is greater than 1.
C 1 is the same as 2.

56. _A_ 1. A random synthesis of molecules on the early earth
2. An enzyme-catalyzed synthesis of molecules on the early earth

57. _B_ 1. Beginning of new life today
2. Beginning of life in the ancient earth

58. _B_ 1. A cell arising spontaneously on the early earth
2. Organic molecules arising spontaneously on the early earth

59. _A_ 1. The first land organisms were plants
2. The first land organisms were animals

60. _B_ 1. The first organic molecule on early earth was an amino acid
2. The first organic molecule on early earth was a protein

61. _C_ 1. Dinosaurs became extinct because severe weather destroyed their food supply
2. Dinosaurs became extinct because the weather became so warm they could not survive

_____

The following four items are based on Miller's experiments on the origins of certain organic compounds. Miller used an electrical discharge through a mixture of gases and noted the resulting products.

62. Miller used the gases NH_3, CH_4, and H_2O in these experiments. He used these gases because they

A contain the atoms necessary to form amino acids.
B are very common molecules found in living organisms.
* C probably existed in the atmosphere of the primitive earth.
D contain carbon, oxygen, hydrogen, and nitrogen.

63. Why did Miller use an electrical discharge as a source of energy?

A Electricity breaks water into oxygen and hydrogen.
B Electricity is used in many chemical experiments.
* C Electrical storms are thought to have been common in the early atmosphere.
D Electrical storms commonly occur today on the earth and on Venus.

64. After one week, Miller analyzed the solution. Amino acids were present. Where did the nitrogen in the amino acids come from?

* A Ammonia
  B Methane
  C Nitrogen gas
  D DNA

65. Which best describes the hypothesis tested in the Miller experiment?

    A Organic compounds can arise spontaneously.
    B Organisms can arise spontaneously.
*   C Organic compounds can be formed under conditions that probably existed in the earth's early atmosphere.
    D Organic compounds need some source of energy for their formation.

The next six items refer to the following chart. The width of each screened area indicates the number of kinds of vertebrates.

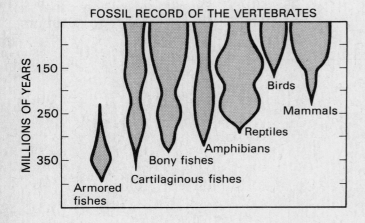

FOSSIL RECORD OF THE VERTEBRATES

66. What is the basis for this chart?

    A The age of fossil mammals
    B The origin of life
    C Carbon dating of the earth's strata
*   D Numbers and geologic ages of fossil species

67. "After an animal group has originated, it tends to develop many kinds." This statement would be classed as

    A a problem.
    B data.
    C a result.
*   D an interpretation.

68. What appears to be the most recent group of animals to have come into existence?

    A Reptiles
    B Mammals
    C Bony fishes
*   D Birds

69. The number of kinds of organisms in a group is a measure of successful adaptation. Which group of fish appears to have been the most successful?

    A Armored fishes
    B Cartilaginous fishes
*   C Bony fishes
    D All groups equally successful

70. On the same basis, which group appears to have been the least successful?

    A Bony fishes
*   B Amphibians
    C Reptiles
    D Birds

71. Variety probably decreases before a group becomes extinct. This idea is shown best by the

    A amphibians.
*   B armored fishes.
    C birds.
    D mammals.

For the next 14 items, determine
the order of Events *1* and *2*.
Select the answer from the Key.

KEY A *1* probably occurred before
        2.
     B *1* probably occurred after
        2.
     C Not enough information is
        available to determine the
        order.

72. _A_ *1.* Carbon dioxide in the
         atmosphere
         2. Green plants

73. _A_ *1.* Ammonia in the atmosphere
         2. Free nitrogen in the at-
         mosphere

74. _B_ *1.* Carbon dioxide in the
         atmosphere
         2. Methane in the atmosphere

75. _B_ *1.* Organisms
         2. Organic molecules

76. _A_ *1.* Amino acid production
         2. Organisms

77. _A_ *1.* Proteins
         2. Life

78. _C_ *1.* Water vapor and hydrogen
         in the atmosphere
         2. Methane and ammonia in
         the atmosphere

79. _A_ *1.* Green plants
         2. Oxygen in the atmosphere

80. _B_ *1.* Life on land
         2. Life in the water

81. _C_ *1.* Microscopic life
         2. Life in the water

82. _A_ *1.* Plants on the land
         2. Animals on the land

83. _A_ *1.* Evolution of amphibians
         2. Evolution of reptiles

84. _B_ *1.* Age of mammals
         2. Age of reptiles

85. _B_ *1.* Evolution of angiosperms
         2. Evolution of gymnosperms

13 Diversity in Form and Function

INFORMATION AND DEFINITIONS

1. In a saltwater environment, the contractile vacuole of *Amoeba* would

    * A be absent.
    B get rid of excess water.
    C get rid of excess salts.
    D serve for locomotion.

2. Suppose the contractile vacuoles of *Paramecium* were removed. Which of the following would happen?

    A They could not eat.
    B They could not move.
    * C They would burst.
    D They would divide in two.

3. What would suggest that an organism seen under a microscope might be an animal?

    A Chloroplasts
    B A cell wall
    C Mitochondria
    * D No cell wall

4. Bacteria usually are classified into three major groups on the basis of

    A size.
    * B shape.
    C protein content.
    D locomotion.

5. What does each colony on an agar plate represent?

    * A A population produced by a single bacterium
    B Bacteria that grouped together when pored on the plate
    C A single bacterium
    D A population of viruses

6. In *Paramecium*, digestion takes place in the

    A surrounding medium followed by absorption.
    * B food vacuoles moving through the cytoplasm.
    C contractile vacuole as it expands and contracts.
    D macronucleus, which controls metabolism and energy transfer.

7. In pond water, protozoa excrete

    A water faster than they take it in.
    B salt faster than they absorb water.
    C water slower than they take it in.
    * D water about as fast as they take it in.

8. *Paramecium* take in food by

    * A sweeping particles into the oral groove.
    B surrounding particles and taking them into the cytoplasm.
    C digesting particles outside the cell and then absorbing the molecules.
    D absorbing only small molecules.

9. Asexual reproduction in *Paramecium* usually results in

    A death of one cell.
    B cells of the same size as the parent.
    * C two identical offspring.
    D two offspring with very different characteristics.

10. *Paramecium* have no nervous system. They behave

    A in a very uncoordinated manner.
    B without reacting to stimuli.
    C uniformly in an unchanging environment.
*   D in a coordinated manner and respond to stimuli.

11. A refrigerator helps prevent food from spoiling because

    A the cold kills bacteria.
    B poisons produced by bacteria are made harmless.
*   C bacterial reproduction is slowed down.
    D bacteria cannot get into food in a refrigerator.

APPLICATION AND INQUIRY

12. Which of the following would you expect to result if the cilia of the oral groove were removed?

*   A The quantity of food particles taken in would be reduced.
    B Action of the contractile vacuoles would be increased.
    C Elimination of wastes would be increased.
    D Reproduction would occur almost immediately but would be abnormal.

The next five items refer to the outline of *Amoeba*. The numbers represent various substances that pass into and out of the cell in fresh water.

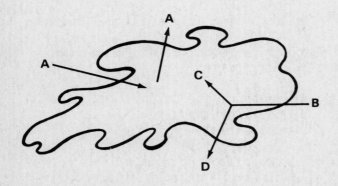

13. Substance A most likely is

    A oxygen.
    B carbon dioxide.
    C fats.
*   D water.

14. The structure involved in handling Substance A is the

*   A contractile vacuole.
    B food vacuole.
    C mitochondrion.
    D nucleus.

15. If Substance B is a protein, then C probably is

*   A amino acid.
    B glucose.
    C carbon dioxide.
    D water.

16. Assume that Substance B is a protein. The structure in the *Amoeba* involved in handling Substance B is the

    A contractile vacuole.
*   B food vacuole.
    C mitochondrion.
    D nucleus.

17. If Substance B is glucose, then Substance D could be

```
*   A   carbon dioxide.
    B   oxygen.
    C   ATP.
    D   starch.
```

_____

The next four items are based on the following experimental design. All the tubes were exposed to normal 24-hour-day conditions.

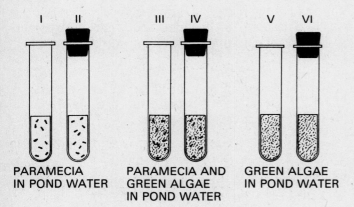

PARAMECIA IN POND WATER

PARAMECIA AND GREEN ALGAE IN POND WATER

GREEN ALGAE IN POND WATER

18. In which tube would carbon dioxide increase most rapidly?

```
    A   I
*   B   II
    C   IV
    D   VI
```

19. Why were stoppered and unstoppered test tubes included? They were used to test whether

```
    A   Paramecium eat green algae.
    B   light is necessary for the
        continuation of life.
*   C   an exchange of gases be-
        tween air and water is
        necessary for life.
    D   Paramecium produce waste
        products.
```

20. In which tube would the organisms die most rapidly?

```
    A   I
*   B   II
    C   III
    D   IV
```

21. Which statement best explains why the organisms in Tubes V and VI live longer than the organisms in the other tubes?

```
    A   Green algae are not affected
        by accumulated wastes.
*   B   Green algae can produce
        their own food.
    C   No other organisms compete
        with algae for food.
    D   The algae grow best by
        themselves.
```

_____

22. Asexual reproduction can be an advantage to *Paramecium*. This is because

```
    A   by this means cells never
        grow old.
*   B   offspring are produced that
        are adapted to the environ-
        ment.
    C   new contractile vacuoles are
        produced with each division.
    D   the cytoplasm of Paramecium
        is renewed continuously.
```

23. The contents of a structure in *Paramecium* were analyzed. They contained 98 percent starch and 2 percent glucose. Contents removed from the same structure three minutes later were 12 percent starch and 88 percent glucose. The data suggest that this structure functions in

```
    A   reproduction.
    B   excretion.
*   C   digestion.
    D   enzyme formation.
```

24. The structure described above moves around within *Paramecium*. Analysis of its contents over time showed a decrease in both sugar and starch and an increase in nitrogen compounds. This suggests which other functions for this structure?

* A Transportation of food and excretion of wastes
  B Exchange of gases and digestion of proteins
  C Transportation of food and exchange of gases
  D Digestion of proteins and excretion of wastes

25. Movement in *Paramecium* is in a forward spiral. This suggests that the *Paramecium* cell is

* A flexible.
  B shaped like a pointed cone.
  C rigid.
  D moved by something other than cilia.

26. *Paramecium* provide a convenient model for studying animal function because

  A their structure is almost identical to that of higher animals.
* B they are easy to grow and observe and carry on basic functions common to all animals.
  C their enzyme systems are easily observed in a laboratory.
  D they are unique in structure and function and offer a contrast to most animals.

27. Sexual reproduction in *Paramecium* involves the exchange of

  A nuclear material between identical individuals.
* B nuclear material between individuals of two mating types.
  C materials between the micronucleus and the macronucleus in one individual.
  D cytoplasmic material between identical individuals.

28. A structure present in a protozoan in fresh water disappears when the protozoan is flooded with salt water. This structure probably controls

  A protein digestion in the cell.
  B salt metabolism in the cell.
* C water content of the cell.
  D movement by the cell.

29. Fission produces two small *Paramecium*. In time, each attains the size of the one that divided to form them. This size increase results from

* A use of molecules from digested food in growth of cell structures.
  B large amounts of water diffusing into the cells.
  C repeated cell division to form a multicellular organism.
  D storage of proteins in special structures of the cell.

The next seven items provide evidence that a particular structure is associated with one of the functions given in the Key. Use the Key to indicate which function most likely is involved.

KEY
- A Removal of excess water
- B Digestion
- C Excretion of fluid wastes
- D Oxygen-carbon dioxide exchange

30. __A__ Removal of the structure causes the organism to swell.

31. __D__ The organism suffocates if the structure is blocked.

32. __B__ The structure is known to convert starch to sugar.

33 __C__ The structure is known to contain urea.

34. __A__ The structure does not function if no water enters the organism.

35. __D__ The structure operates at an increased rate when the organism is very active.

36. __B__ The structure breaks large pieces into small particles by mechanical action.

14   Animal Structure and Function: Digestion

INFORMATION AND DEFINITIONS

1. The process of digestion involves

    A   burning food for energy.
    B   building up protein from
        amino acids.
    C   changing organic molecules.
 * D   breaking large molecules
        into smaller ones.

2. The pancreas is stimulated to
secrete by

    A   food in the mouth.
 * B   food in the small intestine.
    C   the sight and smell of food.
    D   nerve stimulation only.

3. A human blood sample contained
a greater concentration of gastrin
than normal. Food that had been
eaten probably contained

    A   starch.
    B   sugar.
    C   fat.
 * D   protein.

4. Starches can be absorbed after
they have been digested into

 * A   simple sugars.
    B   fatty acids.
    C   proteins.
    D   amino acids.

5. Digestion of proteins produces

 * A   amino acids.
    B   simple starches.
    C   fatty acids.
    D   simple sugars.

6. Molecules that are end products of
digestion are similar in that they

 * A   are water soluble and small
        enough to pass through cell
        membranes.
    B   have long chains of amino
        acids.
    C   contain atoms of C, H, O,
        and N.
    D   are a result of synthesis
        from smaller molecules.

7. The advantage of a tube-type
digestive system is that it

    A   stores large amounts of food.
 * B   permits specialization of
        different regions of the tube.
    C   allows food to pass through
        the organism faster.
    D   insures complete absorption
        of all digested materials.

8. What three secretions mix with the
food in the small intestine?

    A   Saliva, gastric juice, and bile
    B   Gastric juice, bile, and
        pancreatic juice
 * C   Bile, pancreatic juice, and
        intestinal juice
    D   Pancreatic juice, intestinal
        juice, and gastric juice

94

9. How is the small intestine adapted for absorbing digested food?

    A It has a good nerve supply.
    B It has short length.
    C Its muscular walls move the food.
*   D It has folds and villi.

10. When comparing digestion in *Paramecium* and *Hydra*, we find that the process is

    A accomplished by enzymes only in *Hydra*.
    B extracellular in both *Paramecium* and *Hydra*.
    C intracellular in *Paramecium* and extracellular in *Hydra*.
*   D intracellular in *Paramecium* and both extra- and intracellular in *Hydra*.

11. An organism that attaches to fish and sucks blood and body juices most likely would have

    A a long digestive tube with many blind pouches.
*   B a very short, simple digestive tube.
    C no digestive tube.
    D a digestive tube unlike that of any known animal.

12. Any undigested material is ejected from the digestive cavity of *Hydra* through the

    A contractile vacuole.
    B food vacuole.
    C anus.
*   D mouth.

APPLICATION AND INQUIRY

The next four items are based on the following graph. The graph shows the extent to which carbohydrates, proteins, and fats are digested chemically as food passes through the digestive tract. The Roman numerals represent structures in the digestive tract.

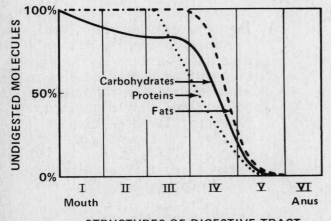

STRUCTURES OF DIGESTIVE TRACT

13. Proteins are digested in both

    A I and II.
    B I and III.
    C II and III.
*   D III and IV.

14. A substance that reacts with fats empties into

    A II.
    B III.
*   C IV.
    D V.

15. The final products of digestion are absorbed almost entirely in

    A II.
    B III.
*   C IV.
    D V.

16. Starch-digesting enzymes are secreted into both

   A I and II.
* B I and IV.
   C II and III.
   D III and IV.

_____

The next six items are based on the following Key to the parts of the human digestive tract.

KEY 1 Mouth
      2 Stomach
      3 Small intestine
      4 Large intestine

17. Which parts have absorption as a chief function?

   A 1 and 2
   B 1 and 3
   C 2 and 3
* D 3 and 4

18. Which parts have digestion as a chief function?

   A 1 and 2 only
   B 1 and 4 only
   C 2 and 3 only
* D 1, 2, and 3

19. In which part is the pH acidic?

   A 1
* B 2
   C 3
   D 4

20. In which part is pancreatic juice added?

   A 1
   B 2
* C 3
   D 4

21. In which part are both salts and water reabsorbed?

   A 1
   B 2
   C 3
* D 4

22. Small food molecules are absorbed primarily in

   A 1.
   B 2.
* C 3.
   D 4.

_____

23. The pH level in the intestine changes from acidic to basic. This change is important to digestion because

   A proteins will not break down in acidic conditions.
   B pepsin activity must stop before intestinal enzymes can become active.
   C intracellular digestion occurs.
* D enzymes secreted into the intestine act best in a basic medium.

24. From an evolutionary point of view, extracellular digestion became necessary as soon as organisms began to feed on each other. Which of the following supports this statement?

   A The more complex the organism, the more complex is its digestive system.
* B Larger food particles can be used in organisms that carry on extracellular digestion.
   C Extracellular digestion enables the organism to become multicellular.
   D Hormonal control of digestion speeds up the evolutionary process.

25. Amino acids were isolated for experimental purposes. Which of the following would be a reasonable experiment to perform with these amino acids?

    A Determine if they came from beef or pork

    B Synthesize fats from chains of amino acids

*   C Synthesize proteins from chains of amino acids

    D Determine their rate of conversion to starch

26. A few organisms apparently cannot digest carbohydrates. Which of the following seems the most logical explanation for this?

*   A No enzymes to digest carbohydrates are present.

    B Cells of these organisms do not use glucose in respiration.

    C These organisms cannot take carbohydrates into their digestive systems.

    D Carbohydrates cannot be synthesized by these organisms.

_____

The two hypotheses below are possible explanations of the control of pancreatic secretion into the intestine.

1. Nerves stimulate the pancreas to secrete its enzymes into the intestine.

2. A hormone in the blood causes the pancreas to secrete its enzymes into the intestine.

Use the Key to classify each of the following seven experiments as they relate to the hypotheses.

KEY A Supports Hypotheses 1 only
      B Supports Hypothesis 2 only
      C Supports both hypotheses
      D Supports neither hypothesis

27. __D__ The pancreas is stimulated when food enters the small intestine of a normal animal.

28. __A__ When a nerve leading to the pancreas is stimulated, the pancreas secretes enzymes.

29. __B__ When the nerves leading to the pancreas are cut and weak acid is placed into the intestine, the pancreas secretes enzymes.

30. __D__ If there is no food in the stomach or intestine of a normal animal, the pancreas will not secrete enzymes.

31. __B__ The blood vessels of two dogs are connected. Food is placed in the intestine of one dog. The pancreases in both dogs secrete enzymes.

32. __A__ If the nerves leading to the pancreas of a hungry dog are cut, the pancreas secretes no enzymes.

33. __A__ The blood from the intestine of an animal is prevented from reaching the pancreas. When the nerve leading to the pancreas is stimulated, the pancreas secretes enzymes.

_____

The next nine items are based on the following data.

Cubes of egg white, a protein, were placed in test tubes containing 10 ml of water. Other substances were added as shown in the chart, and the tubes were left for 12 hours.

Note: Pepsinogen is an inactive substance. Under specific conditions, it is converted to pepsin, an active substance involved in protein digestion.

Which results best support each of the following statements?

TUBE	SUBSTANCE ADDED	POLYPEPTIDES PRESENT	RESULTS
I	Pepsinogen	No	No change
II	Pepsinogen and acid	Large amounts	Clear
III	Nothing	No	No change
IV	Acid	Trace	No change
V	Pepsinogen (boiled) and acid	No	No change
VI	Pepsinogen and base	No	No change
VII	Base	No	No change

34. This tube is the control for the entire experiment.

    A   I
* B III
    C IV
    D VII

35. Protein does not break down spontaneously into polypeptides.

    A   I
* B III
    C V
    D VI

36. Acid breaks down proteins.

    A II
* B IV
    C V
    D VI

37. The pH of the medium is related to the activity of pepsinogen.

    A I and II
* B II and VI
    C II and III
    D V and VII

38. Pepsinogen is involved in enzyme activity.

    A I
    B II
* C V
    D VI

39. The properties of pepsinogen can be destroyed.

    A I
    B II
    C V
    D VI

40. Pepsinogen may be present in small amounts in egg white.

    A I
    B II
* C IV
    D V

41. The conversion of pepsinogen to pepsin appears to be dependent on

* A the presence of an acid.
    B the presence of a base.
    C boiling.
    D time left standing.

42. Suppose finely minced egg white had been used rather than cubes of egg white. In this case,

*   A   the results would have been the same, but the reaction in II would have been faster.
     B   the results would have been the same, but the reaction in II would have been slower.
     C   none of the tubes would have shown the presence of poly-peptides.
     D   all of the tubes would have shown the presence of poly-peptides.

_____

The next five items are based on the following experiment.

A substance was isolated from part of a dog's digestive tract. It was placed into six test tubes arranged in pairs.
     A small amount of cooked potato was added to one pair of tubes. Small chunks of lean meat were added to the second pair. Small chunks of butter were added to the third pair.
     Several drops of HCl (dilute) were added to *one tube of each pair.* All the tubes were kept at body temperature for 12 hours. The only noticeable change occurred in the tube containing the isolated substance, HCl, and meat.

43. This data indicates that the substance came from the dog's

     A   mouth.
     B   large intestine.
*   C   stomach.
     D   small intestine.

44. The substance involved in digestion of the meat was an enzyme that digests

*   A   proteins.
     B   fats.
     C   carbohydrates.
     D   vitamins.

45. A necessary requirement for this enzyme to be active seems to be

     A   dilution.
*   B   presence of an acid.
     C   presence of a base.
     D   salt concentration.

46. If the tubes had been kept at room temperature, the reactions probably would

     A   not have occurred.
*   B   have occurred much slower.
     C   have occurred much faster.
     D   have occurred only in the tube containing butter.

47. Suppose all the tubes had been heated to 100°C and then maintained at body temperature. The reactions would

*   A   not have occurred.
     B   have occurred much slower.
     C   have occurred much faster.
     D   have occurred only in the tubes without acid.

_____

The next four items are based on the
following diagram of the digestive tract
of humans.

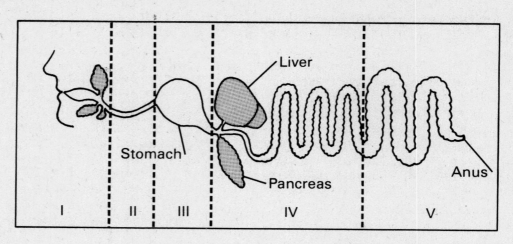

48. The absorption of digested food
takes place almost entirely in

      A   II.
      B   III.
*   C   IV.
      D   V.

49. Two parts of the digestive tract
that secrete starch-digesting enzymes
are

      A I and III.
*   B I and IV.
      C II and IV.
      D III and V.

50. Chemical digestion of protein
occurs in

      A III only.
      B IV only.
*   C III and IV.
      D II and III.

51. An acidic condition normally
is found in

      A   I.
      B   II.
*   C   III.
      D   IV.

15 Animal Structure and Function: Respiration

INFORMATION AND DEFINITIONS

1. Two persons of the same mass produce different quantities of carbon dioxide in the same amount of time. The best explanation for this is that one of them

    A smokes an occasional cigarette.
    B is a woman.
*   C is more active than the other.
    D has not eaten for some time.

2. Breathing is to respiration as

*   A eating is to digestion.
    B plasma is to circulation.
    C enzymes are to synthesis.
    D digestion is to circulation.

3. A person goes from sea level to high altitude. Which is most likely to occur during the first few hours after arrival?

    A Increased number of red blood cells
    B Increased hemoglobin
    C Increased number of white blood cells
*   D Increased breathing rate

4. The function of the air sacs of the lungs is to

*   A provide a large surface area for gas exchange.
    B warm the air before it goes into the circulatory system.
    C filter harmful bacteria out of the air in the lungs.
    D separate the lungs into sections for oxygen and carbon dioxide.

5. Breathing is a mechanical process that provides air for respiration. What systems of the human are directly responsible for breathing?

    A Circulatory and digestive
    B Digestive and skeletal
*   C Muscular and skeletal
    D Muscular and excretory

6. Red blood cells are primarily responsible for

    A clotting the blood.
    B transporting food.
*   C transporting oxygen.
    D killing invading bacteria.

7. In a multicellular organism, which structures are involved most directly in providing oxygen to and removing carbon dioxide from the cells?

    A Capillaries and arteries
    B Arteries and lungs
*   C Capillaries and lung air sacs
    D Lung air sacs and the nasal passage

8. Carbon dioxide leaves hydra and planaria by

*   A simple diffusion.
    B osmosis.
    C evaporation.
    D transpiration.

9. How does a respiratory system provide enough gas diffusion for a multicellular organism such as the human?

* A It increases the surface available for gas exchange.
  B It decreases the surface available for gas exchange.
  C It increases the amount of oxygen needed by the organism.
  D It decreases the amount of oxygen needed by the organism.

10. The grasshopper has an open circulatory system. This system does not permit rapid circulation of body fluids. However, the grasshopper uses large amounts of energy very rapidly. This is possible because

  A it stores oxygen.
  B it does not use oxygen for muscle contraction.
* C its tracheal tubes reach all parts of the body.
  D oxygen is absorbed through the skin.

APPLICATION AND INQUIRY

The next three items are based on the graph of a person's breathing rate. When this person was awake and in a sitting position, the breathing rate was 12 breaths per minute.

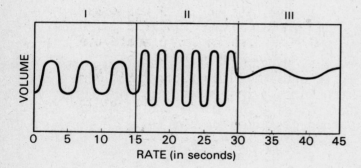

11. Which section of the graph indicates a process of replacing the greatest oxygen deficiency?

  A I
* B II
  C III
  D I and III

12. What would be the order of the sections that demonstrates sleep, climbing stairs, and reading?

  A I, II, III
  B I, III, II
  C III, I, II
* D III, II, I

13. Which section shows the normal breathing rate for this person?

* A I
  B II
  C III
  D II and III

The next three items are based on the following description.

An iron lung consists of a cylinder in which the pressure alternates from higher than atmospheric pressure to lower than atmospheric pressure. A person who has had polio may be put in an iron lung, but his or her head must be outside the cylinder with an airtight seal around the neck.

102

14. The iron lung must replace which of the following in the human?

     A Lungs
     B Bronchial tube
*   C Diaphragm and chest wall
     D Air sacs

15. In the iron lung, the force that pushes air into the human lungs is provided by

*   A atmospheric pressure.
     B the lungs.
     C the iron lung.
     D the diaphragm.

16. The person's whole body could not be put inside the cylinder because

*   A there would be no difference in air pressure inside or outside the body.
     B the pressure difference between the lungs and nose and mouth would be too great.
     C the effect would be bad psychologically.
     D the nasal passage would no longer filter and warm incoming air.

———————————

The next five items are based on the following experimental design.

Five jars were filled with water. All the jars were covered after the following items were added:

Jar 1   Nothing
Jar 2   Two fish
Jar 3   Four fish
Jar 4   Four fish and elodea
Jar 5   Elodea alone

17. Which jar is the control for the experiment?

*   A 1
     B 2
     C 4
     D 5

18. Which jar could be eliminated with the least effect on the experiment?

     A 1
*   B 2
     C 3
     D 4

19. What is the best indirect method of finding the concentration of carbon dioxide in the water? Measure the

     A oxygen content of the water.
*   B pH of the water.
     C photosynthesis of the elodea.
     D change in temperature.

20. If the jars were illuminated, in which jar would the fish live the longest?

     A 2
     B 3
*   C 4
     D 5

21. If the jars were kept in the dark,

*   A the fish in Jar 4 would die before those in Jar 3.
     B the fish in Jar 2 would die before those in Jar 3.
     C the fish in Jar 3 would die before those in Jar 4.
     D the elodea would die but the fish would live.

———————————

22. The hemoglobin molecule has a greater attraction to carbon monoxide than to oxygen. People often die of carbon monoxide poisoning. This happens because the blood's capacity for carrying

*   A oxygen is decreased.
     B oxygen is increased.
     C carbon dioxide is decreased.
     D carbon dioxide is increased.

———————————

The next seven items are based on the following information and graph.

The subject begins by breathing normal air; then 100 percent oxygen; and finally 92 percent oxygen plus 8 percent carbon dioxide. The results appear in the graph.

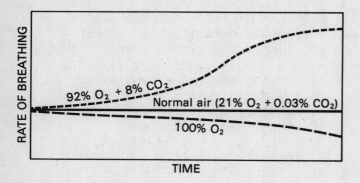

Use the following Key to classify the items.

KEY A Logical hypothesis based on the data
B Hypothesis contradicted by the data
C Hypothesis for which there is *no* data
D Interpretation of the data

23. __D__ The rate of breathing increases markedly in 92 percent oxygen and 8 percent carbon dioxide.

24. __C__ Breathing rate of a rat increases slightly in 100 percent oxygen.

25. __C__ A concentration of more than 8 percent carbon dioxide is fatal.

26. __C__ Temperature is a major factor in increasing the breathing rate.

27. __A__ The concentration of carbon dioxide plays an important part in controlling the rate of breathing.

28. __B__ A high concentration of oxygen is a stimulus to increased breathing rate.

29. __A__ Increased carbon dioxide is a stimulus to increased breathing rate.

_____

The next three items are based on the following observations. A student performed this series of tests:

1 - Exhaled through phenol red solution (an indicator). The indicator turned yellow.
2 - Added acid to phenol red. The indicator turned yellow.
3 - Added water containing CO_2 to phenol red. The indicator turned yellow.
4 - Added acid to clear limewater. The limewater turned cloudy.
5 - Exhaled through clear limewater. The limewater turned cloudy.

30. Based on these tests, which of the following conclusions seems best?

*   A Both limewater and phenol red test for acid.
    B Only limewater is a test for acid.
    C Only phenol red is a test for acid.
    D CO_2 is an acid.

31. If the student is testing for the presence of CO_2 in exhaled air, which of the following is the best conclusion?

    A Phenol red is a test for CO_2.
    B Limewater is a test for CO_2.
    C CO_2 is an acid.
*   D Both phenol red and limewater are tests for CO_2.

32. Which of the following is the best hypothesis to account for these observations?

* A CO_2 combines with water to form an acid.
B CO_2 combines with phenol red to form an acid.
C Limewater combines with CO_2 to form an acid.
D CO_2 changes in the presence of phenol red or limewater.

_____

The next 14 items are based on the following data.

Water fleas, *Daphnia*, are shrimp-like organisms. In water of very low oxygen concentration, *Daphnia* become red. In water high in oxygen concentration, *Daphnia* become colorless.

The plasma of red *Daphnia* is red. The plasma of colorless *Daphnia* is colorless. The red pigment is hemoglobin.

In humans, oxygenated hemoglobin is bright red. Nonoxygenated hemoglobin is dark red. Carbon monoxide-hemoglobin is a bright cherry red, brighter and lighter than oxygenated hemoglobin.

Problem. Carbon monoxide combines with hemoglobin and prevents oxygen from being attached to the molecules. What will happen if carbon monoxide is bubbled through water containing *Daphnia*?

Use the Key to classify the predictions.

KEY A Logical prediction based on all the data
B Prediction contrary to some or all of the data
C Prediction that may be logical but is not based on the data
D Restatement of the data

33. _C_ Lack of oxygen is a stimulus to increase the breathing rate.

34. _A_ The red *Daphnia* will die.

35. _B_ The plasma of the red *Daphnia* will appear blue.

36. _A_ The plasma of the red *Daphnia* will appear bright cherry red.

37. _A_ Most of the hemoglobin will not carry oxygen.

38. _A_ The hemoglobin will turn cherry red.

39. _C_ Carbon monoxide will combine with hemoglobin at the same attachment site as does oxygen.

40. _D_ Hemoglobin is the red pigment in the red *Daphnia*.

41. _D_ Carbon monoxide-hemoglobin is the brightest red of all the hemoglobins.

42. _D_ Oxygen cannot combine with hemoglobin if carbon monoxide is already present.

43. Carbon monoxide did not kill the *Daphnia* when bubbled through the water in which they were kept. What conclusion can be made on the basis of this evidence?

    A Carbon monoxide is not poisonous to human beings.
    B Carbon monoxide does not unite with hemoglobin.
    C The cells of *Daphnia* do not use oxygen.
*   D Hemoglobin is not essential to the life of *Daphnia*.

44. What other piece of evidence supports the conclusion made in the preceding question?

*   A *Daphnia* can be either red or colorless.
    B In the presence of a high concentration of oxygen, *Daphnia* are colorless.
    C In the presence of a low concentration of oxygen, *Daphnia* are red.
    D The plasma of *Daphnia*, when subjected to carbon monoxide, is bright cherry red.

Both red and colorless *Daphnia* were placed in water containing very little oxygen. Both types died, but the red *Daphnia* lived a little longer.

45. What conclusion can be drawn about the role of hemoglobin in *Daphnia*?

    A Necessary and has survival value
    B Necessary but does not have survival value
*   C Not necessary but has survival value
    D Not necessary and has no survival value

46. What inference can be made about hemoglobin in the blood of *Daphnia*?

    A It is always present in the plasma.
    B It moves from plasma to tissue when there is an oxygen deficiency.
    C It is bright red when oxygen is adequate and cherry red when it is not.
*   D It is useful at times of oxygen deficiency.

---

16   Animal Structure and Function: Transportation

INFORMATION AND DEFINITIONS

1. Food molecules are absorbed from the intestine. Then they are carried throughout the body in the

    A white blood cells.
*   B plasma.
    C red blood cells.
    D hemoglobin.

2. The function of the valves in the veins is to

    A decrease blood pressure.
*   B stop backflow of blood.
    C make the flow of blood steadier.
    D slow the flow of blood.

3. The only vessels in the circulatory system across which molecules readily diffuse are

*   A capillaries.
    B veins.
    C arteries.
    D lymph vessels.

4. Lymph nodes and white blood cells are similar in function. Both

    A have multicellular nuclei.
    B are blood cells.
    C contain hemoglobin.
*   D remove harmful bacteria.

5. The work of Harvey and Malpighi showed that

*   A blood circulates.
    B red blood cells carry oxygen.
    C the lymphatic system serves a protective function.
    D blood is formed in the liver.

6. In humans, the wall of the left ventricle is thicker than that of the right ventricle. This adaptation can be explained by the fact that the left ventricle

    A is smaller than the right one.
    B receives only blood low in oxygen content.
    C pumps blood to the lungs.
*   D pumps blood to all parts of the body.

7. Artery walls are more elastic and muscular than the walls of veins. This allows them to

*   A withstand the blood pressure created by the heart's pumping.
    B limit the amount of blood carried by the arteries.
    C insure no loss of blood plasma by diffusion.
    D keep white blood cells from escaping into body fluid.

8. Harvey's hypothesis was not supported totally during his lifetime. This could not happen because

    A the molecular structure of hemoglobin had not been worked out.
    B the function of the lymphatic system was unknown.
*   C a microscope good enough to reveal capillaries had not been developed.
    D it was not known where blood was formed.

9. In hydra, movement of food and waste materials into and out of cells is possible. This can happen because

    A the hydra is a small organism.
    B the cells lining the digestive cavity have flagella.
    C of the action of the hydra's antennae.
*   D nearly all cells are in contact with the watery environment.

10. A function of the lymphatic system is to

    A carry away waste products.
    B carry oxygen to the cells.
*   C transport some harmful substances to lymph nodes.
    D destroy harmful organisms by engulfing them.

11. Red blood cells are responsible primarily for

    A clotting the blood.
    B transporting food.
*   C transporting oxygen.
    D killing invading bacteria.

12. Some animals, such as a hydra, have no special transportation system. This is because

*   A diffusion supplies the cells of the hydra with necessary materials.
    B the cells of the hydra do not need the same materials that other animals need.
    C the hydra's advanced transport system does not need these specialized structures.
    D the hydra uses oxygen dissolved in the water for its transportation system.

APPLICATION AND INQUIRY

The next four items are based on the following data and diagram.

Capillary networks in the tails of a certain species of fish were observed under a microscope. Each specimen was subjected to a series of treatments. Each fish was allowed to recover from the effects of one treatment before being subjected to the next.
    After each treatment, the rate of blood flow was determined. This was done by counting the number of blood cells per minute flowing through ten capillaries.

	TREATMENT	RATE OF BLOOD FLOW
1.	None	600
2.	Adrenaline added (1:10,000 solution)	350
3.	50% alcohol added	810
4.	Lactic acid added (1:10,000 solution)	900
5.	Temperature reduced from 28° to 4°C	300

108

13. The control for this experiment was

*   A 1.
     B 2.
     C 3.
     D 4.

14. Which treatment reduced capillary circulation most?

     A 2
     B 3
     C 4
*   D 5

15. With which treatment did the greatest change in blood flow occur?

     A 2 only
     B 5 only
     C 3 and 4
*   D 4 and 5

16. In selecting treatments for this experiment, the experimenter most likely chose factors

     A that increase heart rate.
     B known to stimulate blood flow.
     C that the fish have in their environment.
*   D thought to influence blood flow.

_____

17. Digested foods are absorbed from the digestive tract at a rate faster than might result from diffusion alone. This suggests that

*   A energy is being expended.
     B muscles are contracting.
     C hormones are being used.
     D food is being broken down by enzymes.

_____

The next three items are based on the following graph.

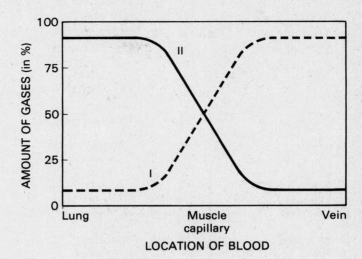

18. In the graph, Line I most likely represents

     A O_2.
     B CO.
*   C CO_2.
     D H_2CO_3.

19. Line II would be lower in the lung region if a person were

     A suffering from loss of white blood cells.
     B running.
*   C on a mountain 13 km above sea level.
     D breathing an atmosphere rich in oxygen.

20. Line I would *not* rise as high in the capillary region of a muscle if a person

*   A were resting.
     B were exercising.
     C had much bicarbonate in the blood.
     D had a slower rate of circulation than normal.

The chart below shows the rate of heartbeat in an animal during activities A-E. Segment A represents the normal heart rate when the animal is awake and relaxed. For each of the seven items below, indicate the segment of the chart that corresponds to the activity.

ACTIVITIES

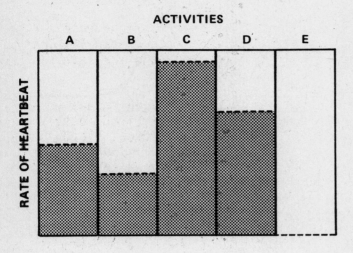

21. _C_ Strenuous exercise such as running upstairs.

22. _B_ Sleep

23. _B_ *Daphnia* subjected to low temperatures

24. _E_ Death

25. _C_ Sudden fright

26. _D_ Light exercise such as walking

27. _D_ Taking a mild stimulant

_____

The next four items are based on a series of experiments.

A heart is removed from the body of an animal. The heart is isolated to determine what factors influence heartbeat.

28. In a saline solution, the heart continues to contract at the same rate. We can assume that the heart

    A requires no energy source.
*   B has internal regulation.
    C depends on body rhythm.
    D grows outside the body.

29. A nerve connected to the heart is stimulated. The rate of contraction slows. This indicates that the heart

*   A responds to nervous control.
    B requires nerve stimulation to speed it up.
    C is controlled by nerve stimulation only.
    D responds differently outside the body than in it.

30. The heart is placed in a saline solution in which other hearts have been slowed by nerve stimulation. Its rate of contraction slows. This indicates that the

    A heartbeat is independent of nervous control.
*   B heartbeat is influenced chemically.
    C heart is poisoned by the solution.
    D heart responds to an adrenaline solution by slowing.

31. The contraction rate is slowed by nerve stimulation and by solutions in which other hearts have been slowed. What is the most logical experiment to perform next?

    A See what chemicals affect heartbeat
    B Determine if the solution contains an enzyme that speeds heart contraction
    C Produce nerveless hearts and repeat the stimulation
*   D Determine any relationship between something in the solution and the nerves

_____

For the next nine items, use the following Key.

KEY The substance listed normally

A passes from the blood, through the capillary wall, and into the fluid that bathes the cells.
B passes from the fluid that bathes the cells, through the capillary wall, and into the bloodstream.
C *does not* pass through the capillary wall.
D passes in either direction through the capillary wall.

32. D Water

33. C Protein molecules

34. D Plasma

35 C Bacteria

36. C Red blood cells

37. B Carbon dioxide

38. A Glucose

39. A Oxygen

40. A Amino acids

———————————

The next ten items are based on the following data. Use the Key to classify the statements.

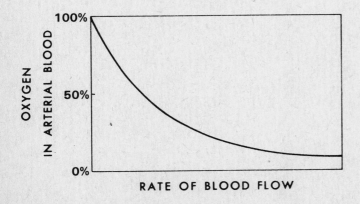

KEY A Logical hypothesis based on the data
B Hypothesis inconsistent with the data
C Correct restatement of the data
D Incorrect restatement of the data

41. B There is no relationship between the oxygen level in the blood and the rate of blood flow.

42. B Lack of oxygen causes contraction of blood vessels and thus reduces blood flow.

43. A Lack of oxygen causes an increase in the size of blood vessels.

44. D 90 percent oxygen in the blood causes a marked increase in blood flow.

45. D Decreasing oxygen has very little effect on the rate of blood flow.

46. D The rate of blood flow decreases as the oxygen level in the blood decreases.

47. C At nearly 100 percent oxygen in the blood, the rate of blood flow is lowest.

48. C As the oxygen level in the blood drops, the rate of flow increases.

49. A Capillaries contract when the percentage of oxygen is high.

50. C The rate of blood flow is inversely proportional to oxygen in the blood.

———————————

51. All nerves to the circulatory system in one leg of an animal are cut. Blood flow to this leg is stopped for one minute. Then it is allowed to start again.

The rate of flow immediately increases. It is two to six times more than what it has been. This rapid flow continues until the cells in the leg are back to normal. What does this experiment indicate?

* A Mechanisms other than nerves also regulate blood flow.
  B Blood ceases to flow between the heart and the leg.
  C Heart rate has changed because the nerves were cut.
  D A hormone slows blood flow through the damaged tissues.

52. Veins that have been over-stretched for long periods of time increase in cross-sectional area. The valves do not increase in size. Therefore, the

  A valves must use twice the energy in transporting blood in the enlarged veins.
  B mass of the blood collapses the valves, making it easier for muscles to return blood to the heart.
  C valves with an increased muscle action will have to return the blood to the heart.
* D valves will no longer block the backward flow of blood in the enlarged veins.

---

17 Animal Structure and Function: Excretion

INFORMATION AND DEFINITIONS

The next four items are based on the following information on excretion. Use the Key to classify the statements.

An amino acid molecule is composed of C, H, O, and N atoms and the energy that bonds them together. These are removed from the body through various routes.

KEY A Skin
     B Kidney
     C Lungs

1. __C__ Where are most compounds containing carbon excreted?

2. __B__ Where are most compounds containing nitrogen excreted?

3. __A__ Where is most heat energy excreted?

4. __B__ Where are most compounds containing hydrogen excreted?

5. Which two major functions do the kidneys perform?

   A They excrete the end products of metabolism and regulate elimination from the digestive tract.
* B They control the concentration of most materials in body fluids and excrete the end products of metabolism.
   C They excrete the end products of metabolism and the substances used in digestion.
   D They excrete the end products of metabolism and regulate secretions from the liver.

6. A homeostatic mechanism

   A maintains a static equilibrium.
* B keeps a system in equilibrium.
   C keeps a system constant or unchanging.
   D maintains identical levels of all hormones.

7. Which of the following mechanisms creates conditions similar to homeostasis in higher animals?

   A Clock
   B Speedometer
   C Telephone
* D Air conditioner

The next seven items are based on the following diagram of a human excretory unit.

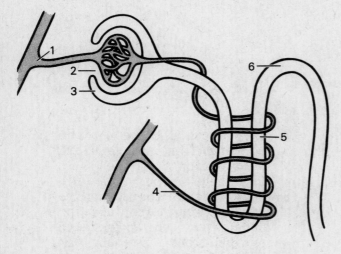

8. The structure into which the filtrate first passes is

    A 1.
    B 2.
* C 3.
    D 5.

9. The structure containing blood with the lowest concentration of urea is

    A 1.
    B 2.
* C 4.
    D 5.

10. The structure that carries urine toward a ureter is

    A 1.
    B 2.
    C 4.
* D 6.

11. The area from which water is reabsorbed is

    A 2.
    B 3.
* C 5.
    D 6.

12. Which substance can be found in 1 but usually is not found in 3?

* A Blood protein
    B Water
    C Glucose
    D Mineral salts

13. The unit shown is a part of the human

    A liver.
* B kidney.
    C lung.
    D heart.

14. In order for glucose molecules to pass from 5 to 4,

    A the glucose must first be broken down.
* B energy must be used.
    C ionization must occur.
    D proteins must be present in 5.

_____

15. Under normal conditions, which substance is completely reabsorbed and returned to the bloodstream by the human kidney?

    A Urea
    B Water
* C Glucose
    D Uric acid

16. Failure of both kidneys in humans usually results in death. This happens because

    A no urea is produced.
* B no urea is excreted.
    C too much water enters the blood.
    D too much water is removed from the blood.

_____

The next [te]n items are based on the
[following] data. Use the Key to
[answer] these statements.

COMPOSITION (grams per 100 ml)			
COMPONENT	PLASMA	FILTRATE	URINE
Urea	0.030	0.030	2.00
Uric acid	0.004	0.004	0.05
Glucose	0.100	0.100	0.00
Amino acids	0.050	0.050	0.00
Salts	0.720	0.720	1.50
Proteins	8.000	0.000	0.00

KEY A Reasonable interpretation
         of the data
     B Interpretation contradicted
         by the data
     C Insufficient information for
         an interpretation

17. __C__ The concentration of cal-
         cium salts is higher in
         the filtrate than in the
         urine.

18. __B__ Glucose is the only compo-
         nent completely reabsorbed
         into the plasma.

19. __C__ Proteins in the plasma break
         down into amino acids in the
         filtrate.

20. __A__ The major substances excreted
         are uric acid, urea, and
         salts.

21. __C__ Glucose is never found in
         the urine.

22. __A__ Filtrate is plasma without
         blood proteins.

23. __A__ Salt concentration in the
         urine is about twice that
         in the filtrate.

24. __C__ The membrane between the
         plasma and the filtrate has
         large pores in it.

25. __B__ Uric acid is the most abun-
         dant component in the urine.

26. __A__ Nitrogen compounds are the
         main ones excreted by the
         kidney.

The next two items are based on the
following information and table.

The filtrate is the fluid that moves
from the blood into the kidney
tubules. Substances in the filtrate
may be reabsorbed, or they may become
part of the urine.

	PARTS PER HUNDRED IN	
SUBSTANCE	FILTRATE	URINE
Protein	0.00	0.00
Glucose	0.10	0.00
Urea	0.03	2.00
Sodium	0.30	0.30

27. Water is reabsorbed from the filtrate. This is supported by the data
on

   A protein.
* B urea.
   C glucose.
   D sodium.

28. Reabsorption of some substances
does occur. This is supported by
the data on

   A protein.
* B glucose.
   C urea.
   D sodium.

29. In what way is the kidney a homeostatic organ?

* A It regulates blood composition.
  B It prevents loss of urea from the bloodstream.
  C It maintains a constant level of tissue fluid.
  D It removes unused nutrients from the body.

_____

The next seven items are based on the following information.

High tides frequently leave behind small ponds of sea water that are about 3 percent salt. As water evaporates, the salt concentration increases two or three times.

In some inland lakes, the salt concentration is even higher. Few organisms can survive in these waters. However, the brine shrimp _Artemia salina_ frequently live in such concentrated salt solutions.

In laboratory experiments, brine shrimp survived in solutions containing from 0.5 to 25 percent salt. The salt concentration in their body fluids always is fairly constant, however, regardless of the water they are in.

30. Most organisms cannot live in salt solutions more concentrated than sea water because

  A most ponds of salty water are too shallow.
* B water is removed from the tissues too rapidly.
  C the high salt concentration increases the water density so the fish float on the surface.
  D water would enter the tissues and the organisms would burst.

Use the following Key to classify the next six items.

KEY A Restatement of the information given
    B Logical hypothesis that might explain the observations and could be tested

31. _A_ Salt concentration in the body fluid of brine shrimp can be different from that of the water they are in.

32. _B_ These animals pump either water or salt to maintain their body contents at a steady level.

33. _B_ These animals carry on active transport of substances out of their bodies, which requires energy.

34. _A_ The salt concentration of these organisms remains quite constant.

35. _A_ These organisms can live in ponds where the salt concentration is over eight times that of sea water.

36. _B_ Many brine shrimp eggs will be laid in an environment in which they cannot develop.

_____

(Note to teacher: The next 45 items refer to the adaptive significance of kidney function and structure for the desert kangaroo rat. Respiration, excretion, adaptation, and evolution are presented in general introductory terms. This series could serve as a basis for classroom discussion.)

Preliminary Observations. The kangaroo rat lives in a burrow by day and comes out to feed at night. It never goes more than a few hundred kilometers from its burrow.

During most of the year, there is no rain in the desert, not even dew. The humidity (water content of the air) usually is near zero percent. In this arid desert, the body of the rat has about the same water content (65 percent of body mass) as that of other mammals.

Many desert animals get their water from plants containing water, such as cactus. But this rat eats dry seeds and dry plant materials.

Problem. How does the kangaroo rat survive in an environment that is almost completely without water?

Use the following Key to classify the statements.

KEY A Hypothesis that can be eliminated on the basis of the information given
     B Logical hypothesis that could be tested
     C Logical hypothesis but unrelated to the problem
     D Not a hypothesis; a restatement of an observation or a statement of a biological principle

37. _B_ The rat manufactures water from the oxygen of the air and from the hydrogen of organic compounds.

38. _B_ The rat gets water through the metabolism of carbohydrates.

39. _A_ The rat takes in water through its respiratory tract.

40. _C_ The chromosome number of the rat's cells will vary from that of its closest relatives.

41. _A_ The dry seeds and vegetation absorb enough water from the air to satisfy the needs of the rat.

42. _D_ The rat does not eat foods with a high water content.

43. _B_ The rat stores water in its body during the infrequent rainy periods in a manner similar to that of the camel.

44. _D_ No animal can live without some source of water.

45. _B_ The rat does not excrete water in its urine and thus conserves water.

46. _A_ The rat obtains water from juicy plants that have a high water content.

Experiment I. Kangaroo rats were collected throughout the year. The water content of their tissues was analyzed. In both the rainy and dry seasons, the total percentage of water in the rats' body tissues was 65 percent.

Use the following Key to classify the hypotheses.

KEY A Illogical hypothesis, but not contradicted by the data
     B Hypothesis that must be rejected on the basis of the data
     C Hypothesis supported by the data
     D Logical hypothesis; but not tested by the experiment

47. _D_ Although the seeds were dry, they had absorbed water before the rat ate them.

48. _A_ The water content in body tissues did not change during the rainy and dry seasons. Therefore, the rats did not consume any of the rain water.

49. __D__ The same amount of water is given off and taken in during both seasons.

50. __D__ The same amount of water is used in tissue construction during both seasons.

51. __C__ The rat does not store water taken in during the rainy season for use during the dry season.

52. __B__ The rat stores water for use during the dry season.

Experiment II. Kangaroo rats were kept in a room at very low humidity. They were fed dry barley seeds and given no water for eight weeks. The percentage of body water at the end of eight weeks was the same as at the beginning even though body mass had increased.

Use the same Key to classify the statements, based on all the information given so far.

53. __C__ The total amount of water in the body of the rat increased.

54. __C__ The percentage of body water remained relatively constant for eight weeks.

55. __D__ More water entered the system than left it.

56. __A__ If water were added to the diet, body mass would increase during the eight weeks.

Experiment III. Kangaroo rats were fed dry barley seeds and watermelon for eight weeks. The percentage of body water remained the same (65 percent) throughout the experiment. These animals had the same increase in mass as did those in Experiment II.

Use the same Key to classify the following statements, based on all of the data presented thus far.

57. __A__ Watermelon was given the rats because they did not know how to drink water.

58. __D__ Wet barley seeds would have given the same results as watermelon and dry barley.

59. __D__ Excess water was eliminated at the same rate that it was taken in.

60. __C__ The rat can maintain a constant water balance regardless of the amount of water in its diet.

61. What conclusion can be made on the basis of the data presented thus far? The kangaroo rat

  A normally eats food that contains enough water to satisfy its needs.
  B manufactures water from hydrogen and oxygen.
* C does not store water when excess water is available.
  D does not need any water.

Review your answers to all the preceding items before interpreting the following experiments.

Experiment IV. In a five-week period, at 50 percent humidity, each rat consumed 100 grams of dry barley. Each rat also excreted about 13 grams of water in urine. About 3 grams were lost in the feces. The total amount of water lost by evaporation from the skin and from the respiratory tract was about 35 grams.

At 50 percent humidity, the barley would contain about 13 grams of water per 100 grams dry mass.

62. About how many grams of water were lost by each rat during the five weeks?

     A   15
     B   35
*   C   50
     D 185

63. About how much water does each rat excrete in five weeks in excess of what it takes in?

     A   3 grams
     B   6 grams
     C 25 grams
*   D 40 grams

Experiment V. When burned (zero percent humidity), 100 grams of dry barley produce 54 grams of water.

Use the Key to classify the following statements.

KEY A Logical prediction based on all the data
       B Illogical prediction
       C Insufficient evidence to evaluate the prediction

64. A More water would be available to the rat as humidity increased.

65. B The intake of water would be between 54 and 67 grams, depending on whether the humidity was 0 or 50 percent.

66. A Water will be available to the rat as a metabolic product.

67. B The rat will have to search for other sources of water.

68. C Young rats use more water than older ones.

69. What evidence is presented that leads to the conclusion that rats use metabolic water?

* A The rats use more water than they take in.
    B They need little water because they live underground.
    C The seeds contain water absorbed from the air.
    D They excrete nitrogen as uric acid.

The following items are based on all the data presented so far. In addition, the following graph shows urea and salt content in human and kangaroo rat urine compared with the salt content of sea water. Use the Key to classify the following hypotheses.

KEY A Illogical hypothesis, but not contradicted by the data
       B Hypothesis that must be rejected on the basis of the data
       C Hypothesis supported by the data
       D Logical hypothesis, but not tested by the experiment

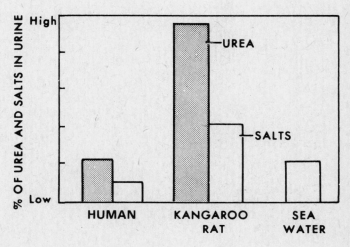

70. __D__ The rat gets most of its water from cellular respiration.

71. __B__ The rat stores water during dry periods.

72. __C__ The rat excretes large amounts of salts and urea in small amounts of water.

73. __D__ Humans cannot drink sea water.

Use this Key to classify the following hypotheses. Base your answers on all the experimental data presented thus far.

KEY A Restatement of the data
       B Logical interpretation of the data
       C Logical prediction
       D False or probably false

74. __D__ The rat stores water in its native habitat but not in the laboratory.

75. __D__ The rat's burrow collects water during the rainy season and this is the rat's only source of water.

76. __B__ The rat can maintain a water balance (ratio of available water to eliminated water) at zero humidity.

77. __C__ If the rat were fed a very high protein diet in the laboratory, more urea would be produced. As a result, more water would be required to eliminate the waste.

78. __C__ If the rat were fed sea water, it could eliminate the salts through the kidney.

79. __A__ There is a higher percentage of urea in the urine of the rat than in the urine of humans.

80. __A__ When water is available to kangaroo rats, they will drink it.

81. __C__ More water is reabsorbed in the kidney tubules of the kangaroo rat than in those of the human.

18 Animal Structure and Function: Coordination

INFORMATION AND DEFINITIONS

1. A sense organ is specialized to receive

    A many types of stimuli.
*   B specific types of stimuli.
    C most changes in the environ-
       ment.
    D coordinated stimuli.

2. Effectors of the [human body that] are controlled by t[he nervous sys-]tem are

*   A muscles and g[lands.]
    B endocrine glands only.
    C body fluids.
    D eyes, ears, and simil[ar]
       sensory parts.

3. A boy of 14 reached a height of 2.1 meters. This probably was caused by an over-secretion of the

    A thyroid gland.
    B adrenal glands.
    C islets of Langerhans.
*   D pituitary gland.

4. Nervous coordination generally differs from endocrine coordination. Nervous coordination is

    A slower.
    B less specific.
*   C faster.
    D controlled by hormones.
_____

Use the Key to classify the next six items.

KEY 1 Adrenal gland
      2 Islets of Langerhans
      3 Parathyroid gland
      4 Pituitary gland
      5 Thyroid gland

5. Produces a hormone that functions in the control of calcium.

    A 1
*   B 3
    C 4
    D 5

6. Produces a hormone that regulates the rate of chemical activities in the cells.

    A 1
    B 2
    C 4
*   D 5

7. May cause diabetes through abnormal functioning.

    A 1
*   B 2
    C 3
    D 4

8. Produces growth hormone.

    A 1
    B 2
*   C 4
    D 5

9. Regulates blood circulation and carbohydrate metabolism.

*   A   1
       B   2
       C   3
       D   4

10. Secretes thyroid-stimulating hormone.

       A   1
       B   2
       C   3
*   D   4

_____

11. In humans, sensory nerves

*   A   carry nerve impulses from receptors to the central nervous system.
       B   carry nerve impulses from the central nervous system to effectors.
       C   move the muscles of the body.
       D   are associated only with sense organs.

12. Associative neurons carry nerve impulses from

       A   motor neurons to sensory neurons.
       B   sensory neurons to muscles.
       C   sensory receptors to the brain.
*   D   sensory neurons to motor neurons.

13. Which activity is increased as a result of diabetes?

       A   Storage of energy for tissue activities
       B   Use of sugar by tissue cells
*   C   Excretion of sugar by the kidneys
       D   Release of insulin from the pancreas

14. The principal effect of thyroxin is to increase the

*   A   chemical activities of all cells.
       B   chemical activities of nerve cells only.
       C   total mass of the body.
       D   amount of sugar in the urine.

15. Impulses pass from one neuron to another

       A   where their cell membranes come in contact.
*   B   across a space between them called a synapse.
       C   where they are joined to the cytoplasm of a receptor.
       D   along the length of the nerve fiber.

16. The part of the brain that regulates breathing is called the

       A   cerebrum.
       B   cerebellum.
*   C   medulla.
       D   spinal cord.

17. A reflex arc is a simple pathway that runs from

*   A   receptor to sensory neuron to associative neuron to effector.
       B   effector to associative neuron to sensory neuron to receptor.
       C   receptor to brain to spinal cord to effector.
       D   one sensory neuron to another.

18. A reflex response in humans can occur without involving

*   A   the brain.
       B   a motor neuron.
       C   a sensory neuron.
       D   an impulse transfer.

_____

The next four items are based on the following diagram and information. The letters A, B, and C represent regions of a human nervous system that might be blocked by a local anesthetic.

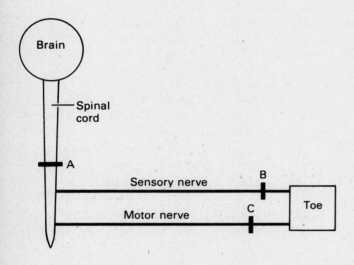

Use the Key to classify the statements.

KEY A Block is at A.
     B Block is at B.
     C Block is at C.
     D No block is present.

19. B The person can move the toe but cannot feel the movement.

20. C The person has feeling in the toe but cannot move it.

21. D When the skin of the toe is stimulated, the toe moves and the person knows it is moving.

22. A When the skin of the toe is stimulated, the toe moves, but the person does not know it is moving.

The next five items are based on the following information.

A "hot foot" results when a match is inserted in the side of a shoe and is lit. Very soon the one receiving the hot foot (1) jerks the leg, (2) feels the pain, and (3) grabs the foot.

23. The first change in the nervous system would be at the

    A sensory neuron.
*   B receptor.
    C motor neuron.
    D muscle.

24. After the stimulus is received, it travels first in the

*   A sensory neuron.
    B spinal cord.
    C brain.
    D motor neuron.

25. Which of the events require a motor neuron?

    A 1 and 2 only
*   B 1 and 3 only
    C 2 and 3 only
    D 1, 2, and 3

26. Which of the events require a functioning brain?

    A 1 and 2 only
    B 1 and 3 only
*   C 2 and 3 only
    D 1, 2, and 3

27. Which of the events is a result of a basic reflex arc?

*   A 1
    B 2
    C 3
    D None of the three

The next six items are based on the following procedure.

Capillary networks in the tails of a certain species of fish were observed under a microscope. Each specimen was subjected to a series of treatments. Each fish was allowed to recover from the effects of one treatment before being subjected to the next.

 After each treatment, the rate of blood flow was determined. This was done by counting the number of blood cells per minute flowing through ten capillaries.

TREATMENT	RATE OF BLOOD FLOW
1. None	600
2. Epinephrine added (1:10,000 solution)	350
3. 50% alcohol added	810
4. Lactic acid added (1:10,000 solution)	900
5. Temperature reduced from 28° to 4°C	300

28. The procedures are an experiment because

    A only sterile materials will be used.
    B quantitative data can be collected.
    C living organisms can be observed.
*   D several trials of different conditions are tested.

29. The capillaries relax and expand in Treatment(s)

    A 2 only.
    B 3 only.
    C 4 and 5 only.
*   D 3 and 4 only.

30. Based on this experiment, one might expect that

    A alcohol would retard blood flow.
*   B extreme cold would decrease circulation to a dog's foot.
    C lactic acid would slow the flow of blood to the tissues.
    D increased epinephrine favors a fear response by increasing blood flow.

31. In the experimental design, Treatment 5 represents a

    A control.
*   B variable.
    C hypothesis.
    D deduction.

32. If a 1:1,000 solution of epinephrine were used, we might predict that the rate of blood flow would

    A increase.
*   B decrease.
    C remain unchanged.
    D level off.

33. The capillaries constrict in Treatment(s)

    A 3 and 4 only.
    B 5 only.
    C 4 only.
*   D 2 and 5 only.

The next five items refer to the following diagram.

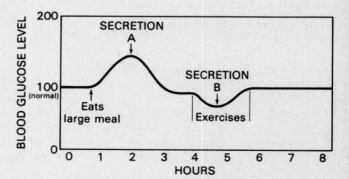

124

34. After this person eats a large meal, the blood sugar goes

    A up, and Secretion A represents epinephrine action.
*   B up, and Secretion A represents insulin action.
    C down, and Secretion A represents epinephrine action.
    D down, and Secretion A represents insulin action.

35. Secretion A brings about

*   A normal blood glucose level in two hours.
    B normal blood glucose level in three hours.
    C increase in blood glucose concentration in two hours.
    D increase in blood glucose concentration in three hours.

36. After the person exercises, the blood glucose level

    A decreases and stimulates Secretion B (insulin).
*   B decreases and stimulates Secretion B (epinephrine).
    C increases and stimulates Secretion B (insulin).
    D increases and stimulates Secretion B (epinephrine).

37. Secretion B brings about normal glucose level in about

    A 5-1/2 hours.
    B 1/2 hour.
*   C 1 hour.
    D 6 hours.

38. The interaction between the secretions and blood glucose is an example of

    A static equilibrium.
    B enzyme control.
*   C homeostasis.
    D a reflex.
    _____

39. Epinephrine is secreted by the ends of neurons. The adrenal glands also secrete epinephrine. Which is the best evidence for this?

    A Epinephrine is a common stimulant in animals.
    B A number of endocrine glands seem to be related to the nervous system.
*   C The area of the adrenal gland that secretes epinephrine is made up of neurons.
    D There is no connection between neuron secretion and epinephrine secretion by the adrenal gland.

40. A nerve in a frog's leg was stimulated electrically. The only reaction was a contraction of the muscle in the same leg. The nerve most likely was

*   A motor only.
    B mixed motor and sensory.
    C sensory only.
    D associative.

41. A child had trouble reading because most of the words appeared backward to the child. What part of the sensory system probably was the cause of this problem?

    A Lens of the eye
    B Retina of the eye
*   C The cerebrum
    D The cerebellum

42. Suppose the cells of a person's pancreas were destroyed. One would expect the concentration of glucose to be

*   A high in both the blood and the urine.
    B normal in the blood and high in the urine.
    C high in the blood and low in the urine.
    D low in the blood and none in the urine.

43. The heartbeat of an isolated heart slows when placed in a solution in which other hearts have been slowed by nerve stimulation. This shows that the heartbeat

    A is independent of nerve control.
* B is influenced chemically.
    C increases in acetycholine solutions.
    D slows in epinephrine solutions.

44. A dog and a frog, sitting on the edge of a cliff, are both touched on the back. The frog jumps headlong into the canyon below. The dog recovers from the surprise in time to stop the first impulse to jump forward. The difference in response of these two animals to the same stimulus can be explained, at least in part. The explanation is that the

    A dog has an endocrine system, but the frog does not.
* B dog has a more complex cerebrum.
    C dog's response is instinctive; the frog's response is learned.
    D dog would be more likely to get hurt by a fall than would the frog.

———————————————

The next nine items refer to the experiment described in the chart. (The presence of thyroxin causes chemical activity in a cell.)

GROUP	EXPERIMENT
A	Control (normal)
B	Daily dose of thyroxin
C	Daily dose of chemical that prevents thyroxin from forming

Use the following Key.

KEY A Group A
      B Group B
      C Group C

In which group would

45. C carbon dioxide production be lowest?

46. C oxygen use be lowest?

47. B metabolic rate be highest?

48. B amount of energy released be highest?

49. A concentration of thyroxin in the blood be medium?

50. B concentration of thyroid-stimulating hormone (TSH) in the blood be lowest? (TSH is produced by the pituitary gland.)

51. B body temperature be highest?

52. C activity of the pituitary gland in producing TSH be highest?

53. B amount of glucose used be highest?

———————————————

The following four items refer to the following diagram.

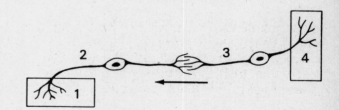

54. Suppose that 1 is a heart and 2 is the vagus nerve. If the vagus nerve were stimulated, what would you expect to find at the junction of 1 and 2?

    A Epinephrine
    B Ion build-up
    C Change in electric properties
* D Acetylcholine

55. Under these conditions, the heart would

     A speed up.
*   B slow down.
     C beat as it did before.
     D stop beating.

56. Suppose that 1 is a heart slowed down by a chemical from 2. In this case, 4 would be the

*   A brain.
     B adrenal gland.
     C pacemaker.
     D aorta.

57. Suppose that 1 is a heart and 2 is the accelerator nerve. In this case, nerve stimulation would cause the heart to

*   A speed up.
     B slow down.
     C beat as it did before.
     D stop beating.

Use the following information to answer the next nine items.

Hypothesis 1. The main function of the parathyroid hormone is to increase the excretion of phosphates into the urine. Other effects are the results of this increase.

Hypothesis 2. The main function of the parathyroid hormone is to cause excessive release of calcium and phosphate from the bones. Other effects are the results of this release.

Use the following Key.

KEY A Supports Hypothesis 1
       B Supports Hypothesis 2
       C Supports both hypotheses
       D Supports neither hypothesis

58. B Bone from newborn mice was placed in tissue culture with parathyroid hormone. The amount of calcium in the tissue culture increased.

59. A Parathyroid hormone was placed in the artery leading to one of a dog's kidneys. More phosphate was found in urine from that kidney than from the other one.

60. D Adding parathyroid hormone increased absorption of calcium from the digestive tract into the bloodstream.

61. B The calcium level of the blood increased when parathyroid hormone was added.

62. A The phosphate level in the blood decreased when parathyroid hormone was added.

63. D Bone contains more than 98 percent of the body's calcium and about 66 percent of its phosphate.

64. A When parathyroid hormone is added, the phosphate level in urine is increased greatly.

65. C An animal's parathyroid glands were removed. The calcium level in its blood was reduced, and almost no calcium was found in its urine. The phosphate level of the blood increased, but the normal amount was excreted.

66. Based on this evidence, where does the parathyroid appear to carry out its action?

     A In the bones only
     B In the kidneys only
*   C In both of these organ systems
     D In neither of these organ systems.

The next 19 items are based on the following data.

Preliminary Data. The hypothalamus is a part of the brain near the pituitary gland. ACTH is a hormone produced by the pituitary. The cortex of each adrenal gland produces another hormone called cortical hormone. A long exposure to a stimulus (cold, pain, and others) is a *stress* stimulus. The table describes a series of experiments involving stress stimuli and ACTH.

EXPER-IMENT NO.	STIMULUS	PITUITARY	HYPOTHALAMUS	SUBSTANCE ADDED	HORMONE PRODUCED BY ADRENAL CORTEX
1	Stress	Normal	Normal	None	Yes
2	Stress	Removed	Normal	None	No
3	Stress	Normal	Injured	None	No
4	None	Removed	Injured	ACTH	Yes

Use the Key to classify the following hypotheses.

KEY A Supported by Experiment 1
     B Supported by Experiment 2
     C Supported by Experiment 3
     D Supported by Experiment 4

67. _C_ The hypothalamus produces a substance that stimulates the adrenal cortex.

68. _D_ This experiment provides evidence that the hypothesis in Item 67 is correct.

69. _B_ The pituitary gland produces a substance that stimulates the cortex of the adrenal gland.

70. _D_ ACTH is a hormone that acts on the adrenal cortex.

71. _A_ Stress is a stimulus for production of ACTH.

Additional Data. The injection of cortical hormone into normal animals has many effects. Among these are increased amount of nitrogen excreted; loss of mass; decreased size of thymus gland; reduced number of white blood cells; and excessive stress causes death. (The thymus gland produces antibodies.)

Three groups of mice were kept under the following experimental conditions.

Group 1. In individual cages; excess food supplied
Group 2. Many in one large cage, but floor space per mouse same as in individual cages; excess food supplied
Group 3. In individual cages on starvation diets

The experimental results are shown in the table.

GROUP	AVERAGE MASS OF ADRENAL GLANDS (mg)	CORTICAL HORMONE IN BLOOD PLASMA (mg/100 ml)
1	3.5	6.5
2	7.5	30.5
3	3.6	6.5

Use the Key to classify the items.

KEY A Logical hypothesis based on the data
     B Illogical hypothesis, or one contradicted by the data
     C Restatement of the experimental results
     D Not a hypothesis and not supported by the experimental results

72. _B_ Lack of food was a stress stimulus.

73. _B_ Lack of space was a stress stimulus.

74. C On the average, the adrenal glands of mice in groups produced more cortical hormone than did the adrenal glands of mice in individual cages.

75. A Interaction with other mice was a stress stimulus.

76. A A direct relationship exists between the stress stimulus and the amount of cortical hormone produced.

77. D A mouse in a single cage produced about the same amount of cortical hormone as the most dominant member of the large group.

78. A A behavioral mechanism operates to control populations.

79. D The individuals lowest in the social order produce the least cortical hormone.

80. B Increased social pressure increases the population.

81. D Famine and predators are the principal factors in limiting populations.

82. A Aggression and competition are stress stimuli.

83. B The density of the population, rather than the number of interactions between individuals, is the important factor in regulating population growth.

84. D Birthrate increases with an increase in cortical hormone.

85. D Death rate decreases as population increases.

_____

The next two items are based on the following diagram of a reflex arc. The arrows show the direction of impulses.

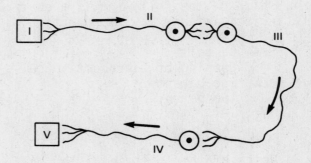

86. A muscle or gland is most likely to be found at

    A I.
    B II.
    C III.
*   D V.

87. A sensory neuron is represented by

*   A II.
    B III.
    C IV.
    D V.

19 Animal Structure and Function: Reproduction

INFORMATION AND DEFINITIONS

1. Which of the following is a characteristic of asexual reproduction?

    A Meiosis
    B Uniting of reproductive cells
*   C One parent
    D Two parents

2. Which of the following is *not* a form of asexual reproduction?

*   A Conjugation
     B Budding
     C Parthenogenesis
     D Cloning

3. Fertilization is a process by which

    A cells divide to produce more cells.
*   B nuclei of two separate cells unite into one.
    C organisms at all levels of complexity reproduce.
    D mitosis occurs to produce more cells.

4. Reproduction is a process of greatest value to the

*   A species.
    B individual.
    C environment.
    D population.

5. Human sperm and eggs are similar in which of the following ways?

    A They have about the same mass.
    B The number produced is about the same in both.
    C They are both motile.
*   D They have the same number of chromosomes.

6. Male deer have antlers, roosters have heavier combs than hens, male birds have striking differences in colors. These differences are due in part to

    A thyroxin.
    B epinephrine.
    C estrogen.
*   D testosterone.

7. Sexual reproduction is more important to evolution than is asexual reproduction. This is because sexual reproduction

*   A provides for variety among offspring.
    B serves better to perpetuate the species.
    C produces offspring identical to the parents.
    D ensures less variety in genetic types.

8. Male and female organisms can be identified best by

    A their relative sizes.
    B the amount of body coloration.
* C the reproductive cells they produce.
    D the amount of muscles they have.

9. Reproduction differs from all other functions in an organism because it is not

    A an energy-consuming process.
* B necessary for the individual to live.
    C a normal body function.
    D important to the organism's species.

APPLICATION AND INQUIRY

The next four items are based on the diagram of the menstrual cycle.

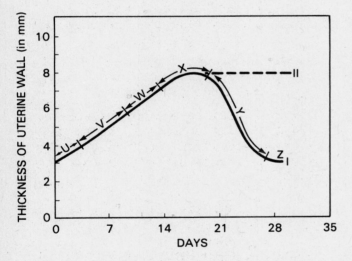

10. Line II would be expected if

    A the lining of the uterus were shed.
* B embryo attachment occurred.
    C progesterone decreased.
    D the corpus luteum degenerated.

11. During which segment of the cycle is ovulation most likely to occur?

    A U
* B W
    C Y
    D Z

12. Which would be expected to occur during Segment Y?

    A Follicle will secrete estrogen.
    B Follicle will rupture.
    C Secretion of progesterone will be at a maximum.
* D Corpus luteum will degenerate.

13. Segment V is primarily under the influence of

* A estrogen.
    B progesterone.
    C epinephrine.
    D testosterone.

14. When the pituitary is removed from immature female rabbits, their ovaries do not develop normally. When the pituitary is removed from mature female rabbits, the ovaries and uterus stop functioning. What do these observations alone indicate?

    A The ovaries influence the uterus.
* B The pituitary influences the ovaries and uterus.
    C The ovaries and uterus influence the pituitary.
    D Hormones feed back from the ovaries to the pituitary.

The rats described in the following table were used in a series of experiments to determine the relationship among the pituitary gland, the ovaries, and the uterus.

RAT	PITUITARY	OVARIES	UTERUS
I	Removed	Present	Present
II	Removed	Removed	Present
III	Present	Removed	Present
IV	Present	Removed	Removed
V	Removed	Present	Removed

Use the Key to classify the next 12 hypotheses.

KEY A Supported by the data
     B Contradicted by the data
     C Neither supported nor
        contradicted by the data

Experiment 1. Pituitary extract was injected into Rat I. As a result, an ovary produced a follicle and the uterus enlarged.

15. _A_ The pituitary affects the ovaries.

16. _A_ The pituitary affects the uterus.

17. _C_ The ovaries affect the uterus.

18. _C_ The ovaries affect the pituitary gland.

19. _C_ The uterus affects the pituitary gland.

Experiment 2. Pituitary extract was injected into Rat II. The uterus did not enlarge. (Use only the results of Experiment 2 to classify the next three hypotheses.)

20. _C_ The pituitary gland affects the ovaries.

21. _B_ The pituitary gland affects the uterus.

22. _C_ The uterus affects the pituitary gland.

Experiment 3. Ovary extract was injected into Rat III. The uterus enlarged. The pituitary did not change in size, but there was a change in hormone production. (Use only the results of Experiment 3 to classify the following three hypotheses.)

23. _A_ The ovaries influence the uterus.

24. _C_ The uterus influences the ovaries.

25. _A_ The ovaries influence the pituitary gland.

26. What experiment would test whether the uterus influences the pituitary gland?

*   A Uterus extract injected into Rat IV
     B Uterus extract injected into Rat V
     C Pituitary extract injected into Rat IV
     D Pituitary extract injected into Rat V

The next eight items are based on the following graph of the human menstrual cycle. On it are plotted the amounts of three hormones-- estrogen, progesterone, and LH--as well as the thickness of the wall of the uterus.

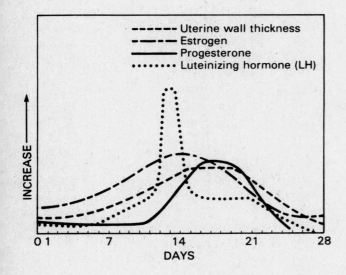

----- Uterine wall thickness
--·-- Estrogen
——— Progesterone
······· Luteinizing hormone (LH)

27. In this cycle, the release of an egg occurs

    A between Day 16 and Day 26.
* B between Day 12 and Day 16.
    C on Day 10.
    D on Day 28.

28. Which of the following is a function of progesterone?

* A It prepares the uterus to receive the egg.
    B It stimulates ovulation.
    C It stimulates estrogen production.
    D It stimulates the corpus luteum.

29. Menstruation begins when

    A LH activity is at its peak.
    B estrogen activity reaches its peak.
    C progesterone activity is at its highest.
* D progesterone and estrogen activity are declining.

30. After ovulation, the egg lives only a few days. If it is not fertilized, it disintegrates. Knowing this, you could predict that the greatest possibility of pregnancy occurs between

    A 0 and 6 days.
    B 6 and 10 days.
* C 12 and 18 days.
    D 22 and 28 days.

31. The uterus would be most prepared to receive the fertilized egg during the period between

    A 0 and 12 days.
    B 12 and 16 days.
* C 16 and 22 days.
    D 0 and 28 days (the entire cycle).

32. Progesterone secretion decreases sharply near the end of the cycle because

* A the corpus luteum degenerates.
    B the corpus luteum appears.
    C ovulation occurs.
    D pregnancy results.

33. The hormone levels in the normal menstrual cycle are controlled by the

    A uterus only.
    B ovaries only.
    C uterus and ovaries.
* D ovaries and pituitary gland.

34. The increase in estrogen activity is due to

* A FSH stimulation of the ovaries.
    B LH activity.
    C LH secretion by the pituitary.
    D increase in size of the uterus.

For the next five items, compare sexual and asexual reproduction using the following Key.

KEY A Sexual reproduction
     B Asexual reproduction
     C Both of these
     D Neither of these

35. __C__ A new individual develops from a single cell.

36. __B__ A willow tree develops from a cutting.

37. __A__ Two gamete nuclei unite.

38. __A__ Chromosomes separate by meiosis.

39. __B__ The offspring are exactly like the parents.

_____

40. A nuclear change is necessary for sexual reproduction. This change is the

        A development of a new indi-
           vidual from a single cell.
*   B reduced number of chromosomes
           in gametes.
        C doubling of the chromosome
           number in gametes.
        D development of gametes with
           the same chromosome number
           as in the body cells of the
           species.

41. Bird's eggs contain more yolk than do mammalian eggs. This indi-cates that

        A birds need more energy for
           development.
*   B mammals do not depend totally
           on the yolk for development.
        C birds develop slower and
           need more energy.
        D the yolk of mammals is more
           concentrated.

42. In some placental mammals, the ovaries can be removed during preg-nancy without affecting development of the embryo. This suggests that

*   A something other than the
           ovaries maintains the uterus
           during pregnancy.
        B the ovaries need not be
           present for an animal to
           become pregnant.
        C the ovaries influence the
           uterus through hormones.
        D pituitary glands influence
           the period of pregnancy.

43. Species A reproduces by mitosis. Species B reproduces sexually. All other characteristics are similar in the two species. When the environ-ment changes,

        A both species should have an
           equal chance of surviving.
        B Species A should have a
           better chance of surviving
           than Species B.
*   C Species B should have a
           better chance of surviving
           than Species A.
        D Neither species would sur-
           vive, since organisms often
           become extinct if the environ-
           ment changes.

_____

The next five items are based on the following diagram of the male repro-ductive system.

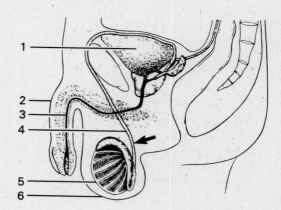

44. The structure that produces sperm is

    A 2.
    B 3.
    C 4.
*   D 5.

45. The structure used by both the reproductive and urinary systems is

    A 2.
*   B 3.
    C 4.
    D 5.

46. The structure that changes size when stimulated is

    A 1.
*   B 2.
    C 3.
    D 4.

47. The structure that produces hormones is

    A 1.
    B 2.
    C 4.
*   D 5.

48. If Structure 4 were tied off at the arrow, which of the following would occur?

    A No sperm would be produced.
*   B Sperm could not be carried to the outside of the body.
    C Urine could not be discharged from the bladder.
    D Sex hormones would no longer be produced.

———————————

The next seven items are based on the following diagram of the female reproductive system.

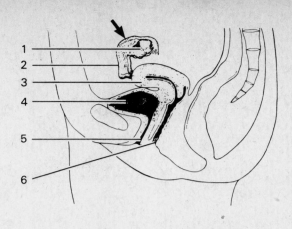

49. Eggs are produced in

*   A 1.
    B 2.
    C 3.
    D 4.

50. The human embryo develops in

    A 2.
*   B 3.
    C 4.
    D 5.

51. The structures used by the urinary system are

    A 1 and 2.
    B 2 and 3.
*   C 4 and 5.
    D 5 and 6.

52. The menstrual flow comes from the wall of

    A 1.
*   B 3.
    C 4.
    D 6.

53. Fertilization of the human egg occurs in

    A 1.
*   B 2.
    C 4.
    D 6.

54. Which structures are most closely involved in the actual birth of a baby?

       A 4 and 5
       B 1 and 6
*   C 3 and 6
       D 2 and 5

55. If Structure 2 were tied off at the arrow

*   A eggs would not reach the uterus.
       B the corpus luteum could not produce progesterone.
       C urine could not be discharged.
       D a pregnancy in progress would be stopped.

The next five items are based on the following reading.

In several families of tropical fish, sex reversal is common. It has been observed in the "cleaner fish," *Labroides dimidiatus*. A research team studied 11 groups of *Labroides*. Each group had one adult male, three to six adult females, and a few immature females. The male defended a territory. There was a social hierarchy of male, Female 1, Female 2, Female 3, and so on. The females had individual feeding areas within the territory.

Occasionally, one of the males died. Within one to two hours, Female 1 in that group showed aggressive behavior typical of the male. Within two to four days, she exhibited male mating behavior. Fourteen to 18 days after the beginning of this sex reversal, the new "male" could produce sperm.

Would removing the male from the group cause sex reversal in Female 1? In 21 instances of removing the male, Female 1 always underwent sex reversal.

If a male were placed in the group as a new "male" was developing, would the new "male" continue the reversal? In four cases, the new "male" did not complete the change. She again became a fully functioning female. And the introduced male took over control of the group.

In the fifth case, however, things went differently. An original male died. Another male was introduced. Female 1 went through three changes: she became a new "male," then a female, and then a new "male." After this final change, the new "male" chased the introduced male from the territory.

56. Which of the following questions was answered when a male was introduced into a group where a female was undergoing sex reversal?

*   A Can a female in the process of becoming a new "male" change back into a functioning female?
       B Will a male introduced into a group having a functioning male become a functioning female?
       C Does sex reversal in females occur during some seasons but not others?
       D In situations of environmental stress, will both Female 1 and Female 2 become new "males"?

57. If both the male and Female 1 were removed from the territorial group, you could expect that

    A the group would remain without a male.
    B the remaining females would leave and join neighboring groups.
*   C Female 2 would begin reversal to male form.
    D an extra male from another group would take over.

58. The most convincing evidence for actual sex reversal is the new "male's"

    A external appearance.
    B aggressive behavior.
*   C production of sperm.
    D courtship behavior.

59. The stimulus for production of a new "male" seems to be

*   A absence of a male in the territorial group.
    B aggression by males from other groups.
    C overabundance of females within the territorial group.
    D availability of unused feeding areas.

60. What is the possible advantage to the species of this pattern of sex reversal?

    A It maintains a constant population size within the group territory.
    B It insures that all offspring are genetically identical.
*   C It favors genotypes successful in the group territory.
    D It prevents an overabundance of aggressive males.

20 Photosynthesis and Plants

INFORMATION AND DEFINITIONS

1. Suppose all green plants were to disappear suddenly. Which of the following substances, normally found in the atmosphere, probably would be used up first?

    A CO_2

    B N_2

    C H_2O vapor

*   D O_2

2. Which isotope most logically would be used to study the dark reactions of photosynthesis?

    A $Hydrogen^3$

    B $Sulfur^{35}$

*   C $Carbon^{14}$

    D $Oxygen^{18}$

3. Respiration is to carbon dioxide as photosynthesis is to

    A carbon dioxide.

*   B oxygen.

    C light.

    D nitrogen.

4. Which occurs during the dark reactions in photosynthesis?

    A ATP is produced in the mitochondria.

    B Chlorophyll releases energy.

    C Water releases hydrogen.

*   D Carbohydrate molecules are synthesized.

5. As a result of photosynthesis, oxygen is given off by the green plants. This oxygen comes from

    A CO_2.

*   B H_2O.

    C $C_6H_{12}O_6$.

    D H_2CO_3.

6. Several plants are grown at various wavelengths of light. You would expect the greatest growth in those grown in

    A violet and ultraviolet light.

    B green light only.

*   C red and blue light.

    D yellow and orange light.

———————————————

The next five items refer to comparisons of light and dark reactions in photosynthesis. Use the following Key.

KEY Occurs in

    A light reactions

    B dark reactions

    C both sets of reactions

    D neither set of reactions

7. __A__ Radiant energy is absorbed by chlorophyll.

8. __D__ Carbon dioxide is broken down.

9. _C_ Reactions are catalyzed by enzymes.

10. _A_ Oxygen is produced.

11. _A_ ATP is produced.
_____

12. Carbon dioxide enters a leaf from the air outside because

*   A its concentration is greater in the outside air than in the leaf.
    B it is drawn in by the movement of guard cells.
    C it is needed for photosynthesis.
    D plants use carbon dioxide or give off oxygen.

13. At the end of the season, the dry mass of a hectare of corn plants is nearly six metric tons. Most of this dry mass consists of

    A minerals from soil.
*   B carbon dioxide from air and water from soil.
    C water and minerals from soil and oxygen from air.
    D carbon dioxide and water vapor from air.

14. The loss of water by a green plant is controlled mainly by

*   A guard cells.
    B palisade cells.
    C epidermal cells.
    D spongy layer cells.

15. Which of the following will cause leaf stomates to open?

*   A Water molecules move into guard cells.
    B The air around the leaf becomes less humid.
    C Salt molecules are excreted from the guard cells.
    D Glucose molecules are converted to starch.

Use the following Key to answer the next ten items about the function of leaf parts.

KEY

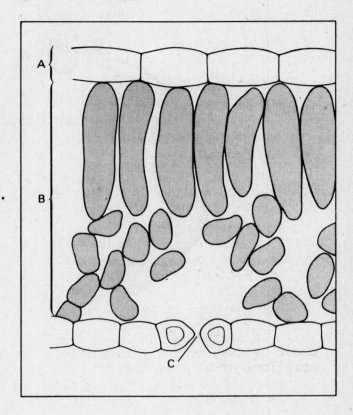

16. _C_ Where carbon dioxide enters the leaf

17. _B_ Where carbon dioxide is used

18. _B_ Where photosynthesis occurs

19. _A_ Where wax surface may be produced

20. _B_ Where glucose is produced

21. _C_ Where most of the water leaves the leaf

22. _B_ Where oxygen is produced

23. _C_ Where oxygen leaves the leaf

24. _B_ Where there are many chloroplasts.

25. <u>A</u> Where most of the light
        energy enters

_____

2 (26.) The primary function of xylem
     and phloem is

        A absorption.
        B storage.
    *   C conduction.
        D photosynthesis.

3 (27.) The plant tissue specialized for
     continued mitosis is called

        A pith.
        B xylem.
    *   C cambium.
        D bark.

4 (28.) The chief supporting cells of a
     woody plant stem are found in the
     gymnosperm

        A bark.
    *   B xylem.
        C phloem.
        D cambium.

5 (29.) The primary function of living
     phloem is conducting

    *   A soluble foods.
        B dissolved minerals.
        C oxygen and carbon dioxide.
        D water.

6 (30.) In a ~~very~~ woody stem, which of
     the following tissues would be most
     abundant?

    *   A Xylem
        B Pith
        C Cambium
        D Phloem

7 (31.) The diameter of a woody plant stem
     increases due to cell division in the

        A xylem.
        B phloem.
        C bark.
    *   D cambium.

32. Glucose will flow out of roots
only if there is

        A active transport.
    *   B death of the plant.
        C a negative pressure in the
           roots.
        D starch in the soil around
           the roots.

33. Which of the following is absorbed through the root hairs of
plants?

        A Proteins
        B Carbohydrates
    *   C Oxygen
        D Carbon dioxide

34. Carbon dioxide is to stomates
as water is to

        A xylem.
        B osmosis.
    *   C root hairs.
        D bark.

35. A plant has thick, fleshy stems,
few or no leaves, and an extensive
root system. This plant probably
grows in a climate that is

    *   A dry.
        B humid.
        C hot.
        D cold.

_____

Classify the next ten items using
the following Key.

KEY A Respiration
     B Photosynthesis
     C Both of these
     D Neither of these

36. <u>A</u> Occurs at all times in plants

37. <u>C</u> Occurs in the light in plants

38. <u>A</u> Produces carbon dioxide

39. <u>B</u> Uses carbon dioxide

140

40. __D__ Produces amino acids

41. __C__ Involves an energy change in molecules

42. __B__ Involves dark reactions and light reactions

43. __C__ Involves enzymes in the reactions

44. __A__ Occurs in mitochondria

45. __C__ Occurs in chloroplasts

APPLICATION AND INQUIRY

The next eight items refer to an experiment with five geranium plants. The plants were treated as shown in the tables

Placed in the Light

PLANT	TREATMENT	RESULTS
1	Half of each leaf covered with aluminum foil	Half exposed to light had no starch
2	Upper and lower surfaces of leaves covered with petroleum jelly	No starch
3	Placed in jar containing no carbon dioxide	No starch

Placed in the Dark

PLANT	TREATMENT	RESULTS
4	Leaves removed and placed with petioles immersed in glucose solution	Starch, especially in veins of leaves
5	No treatment	No starch

Use the following Key to classify the statements below.

KEY   The interpretation is

A   rejected on the basis of the data.
B   supported by the data.
C   logical, but the experiment does not test it.

46. __B__ The presence of starch indicates photosynthesis only if the leaf is deprived of an outside source of glucose.

47. __C__ Starch may diffuse from its site of origin throughout a leaf. Thus, its location does not indicate where it was formed.

48. __A__ Light is necessary for starch formation in plants.

49. __B__ Glucose is necessary for starch formation in plants.

50. __B__ Plant 2 had no carbon dioxide intake because the stomates were covered.

51. __C__ The roots of a plant may store starch.

141

52. What assumption must be made in order to interpret the results of this experiment? The assumption is

    A only that the presence of starch indicates that photosynthesis has taken place.
    B only that the petroleum jelly will not cut out light.
*   C both A and B.
    D neither A nor B.

53. What was the control for Plant 2?

    A Plant 1--covered part
    B Plant 1--uncovered part
    C Plant 3
*   D No specific control

----

54. A certain plant species has leaves that are partly green and partly white. Iodine tests always show starch in the green parts and none in the white parts. One could hypothesize that

*   A chlorophyll is necessary for starch production.
    B starch in the white parts does not respond to iodine.
    C starch is turned to sugar rapidly in the presence of chlorophyll.
    D the white parts of the leaves produce sugar.

55. Green leaves were kept in the dark for several days. Then they were tested for starch, and no starch was found. What hypothesis would this investigation test?

    A Starch turns to sugar.
*   B Light is necessary for starch production.
    C Plants store starch in their roots.
    D Chlorophyll uses starch for food.

56. A plant was kept in the dark for several days. Then it was exposed to radioactive carbon dioxide for a few minutes. One would expect to find that

    A the compounds formed were not radioactive.
    B traces of carbohydrate were to small to identify.
*   C carbon in some of the carbohydrates was radioactive.
    D only a small amount of glucose was produced.

The next four items refer to the following graph.

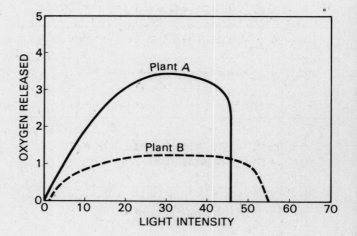

57. Photosynthesis is expressed here in terms of the amount of oxygen released per hour by the plant. It is expressed this way mainly because oxygen

    A combines readily with most substances.
    B is the principal product of photosynthesis.
*   C is a measurable by-product of photosynthesis.
    D is released constantly by all plants.

58. Plant A would be better suited than Plant B for living in

    A artificial light.
    B light of an intensity of 50.
    C light of all intensities.
* D the shade.

59. Which situation probably would release the greatest amount of oxygen?

    A Plant A in the dark
* B Plant A at a light intensity of 30
    C Plant B in the dark
    D Plant B at a light intensity of 40

60. Which situation probably would release the greatest amount of carbon dioxide?

    A Plant A in the dark
    B Plant B in the dark
    C Plant A at a light intensity of 30
* D Impossible to tell from the data

———————————————

The next five items refer to the following information and graph.

An immersed water plant was exposed to light of gradually increasing intensity for several hours. At regular intervals, the number of bubbles released in one minute were counted.

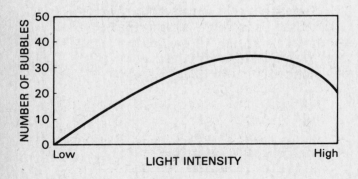

Use the following Key for the next three items.

KEY A Logical interpretation of the data
       B Restatement of the data

61. <u>A</u> The light could be increased to an intensity that would prevent photosynthesis.

62. <u>B</u> A maximum of 35 bubbles per minute was recorded.

63. <u>A</u> There is an optimum range of light intensities for photosynthesis.

64. The number of bubbles released apparently was

    A directly proportional to light intensity throughout the experiment.
    B causing light to become more intense as the experiment progressed.
    C decreased halfway through the experiment.
* D correlated with light intensity during most of the experiment.

65. The release of bubbles is most useful as an indication of the rate of

    A growth.
* B photosynthesis.
    C metabolism.
    D active transport.

———————————————

The next seven items are based on the following experiment.

Some students exposed a corn plant to light for two hours. They placed some of the leaves from this plant in a test tube and added a little water. Then they added Fehling's solution, which turns red when in contact with a hot glucose solution.

The students heated the contents of the test tube to the boiling point. The solution became red. They concluded that the leaves had produced glucose by photosynthesis.

To reach this conclusion, they made some assumptions. Use the following Key to classify the assumptions.

KEY A Justifiable and necessary assumption
     B Justifiable but unnecessary assumption
     C Unjustified or irrelevant assumption
     D Not an assumption, a restatement of results

66. _C_ Glucose is formed most abundantly in leaves.

67. _B_ Some other types of leaves will give the same results as those described.

68. _B_ Only green leaves will give a positive test for glucose.

69. _A_ Fehling's solution will not turn red when boiled with pure water.

70. _A_ A glucose solution will not turn red spontaneously.

71. _A_ The color from the leaves did not affect the test for glucose.

72. _D_ The solution turned red after boiling.

The next three items are based on the following diagram. The diagram shows the rates of photosynthesis in varying amounts of light and carbon dioxide.

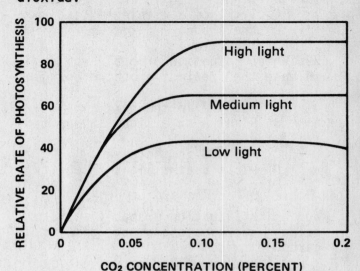

73. The lowest CO_2 concentration that will produce the highest photosynthetic rate at any light intensity is

    A 0.05%.
*   B 0.10%.
    C 0.15%.
    D 0.20%.

74. The normal CO_2 concentration in the atmosphere is 0.04%. If the data in the graph are correct, plants in full sunlight are photosynthesizing

*   A at less than maximum rate.
    B faster than they should.
    C at the maximum rate.
    D faster than the experimental plant in low light.

75. Suppose you wanted to prevent photosynthesis in a plant in full sunlight. It would be best to put the plant in a container with a CO_2 concentration of

*   A 0.0%.
    B 0.05%.
    C 0.10%.
    D 0.20%.

The next five items are based on the following experiment.

Some water, soil, and a few green aquatic plants were placed in a large bottle with a fish. The bottle was sealed to prevent the exchange of gases and other materials with the outside environment. It was then placed where it received light during the day.

76. Will carbon dioxide be used by the plants?

   A No, carbon dioxide is a waste product of respiration.
   B Yes, it will be used 24 hours a day during photosynthesis.
   C Yes, it will be used all the time in respiration.
*   D Yes, it will be used in the daytime during photosynthesis.

77. Will oxygen be used by the plants?

   A No, oxygen is produced, not used, by plants.
   B Yes, it will be used 24 hours a day during photosynthesis.
*   C Yes, it will be used all the time in respiration.
   D Yes, it will be used at night after photosynthesis is ended.

78. Will oxygen be used by the fish?

*   A Yes, it will be used 24 hours a day in respiration.
   B Yes, but only at night after photosynthesis has ended.
   C Yes, but only in the daytime during photosynthesis.
   D No, the fish will give off oxygen as a waste product from metabolism.

79. The immediate source of energy for the fish will be

   A sunlight absorbed through its body.
   B glucose metabolism.
*   C ATP stored in the mitochondria.
   D fats stored among body tissues.

80. Will carbon dioxide be produced by the plants?

   A Yes, but only at night when the plants no longer can carry on photosynthesis.
*   B Yes, it will be produced all the time as a result of respiration.
   C No, it is a waste product of animals only.
   D No, plants take in only the waste products exhaled by animals.

_____

For the next seven items, assume that Plants X and Y normally grow in a temperate climate. The graph shows the water loss from the leaf surfaces for both plants in a temperate area.

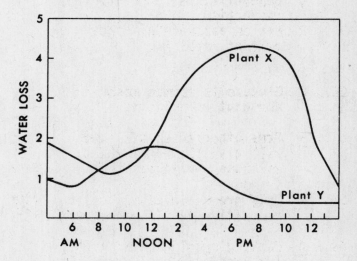

Use the Key to indicate what would happen if these plants were grown under the conditions described in the following statements. (Consider water loss from leaf surface as the important factor.)

KEY A Y is more likely to survive than X.
      B X is more likely to survive than Y.
      C Both are likely to survive.

81. _C_ In a humid environment

82. _A_ In a dry environment

83. _C_ In a tropical forest

84. _C_ in a swamp environment

85. _A_ In a windy environment

86. _A_ If root surface is small

87. _C_ If root surface is large

The next six items are based on the following experiment.

Four cuttings were made from one plant. The cut end of each stem was inserted into a glass tube. The tube was placed in a flask of water. Movement of water into the stem was shown by movement of water up the tube.

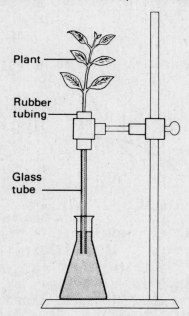

Plant

Rubber tubing

Glass tube

The four setups received the following treatments.

Transpirometer

A	Left in room light
B	Placed in sunny window
C	Placed in the dark
D	All leaves removed

88. The function of a transpirometer is to measure

    A the pressure of water entering the roots.
    B transpiration as it occurs in the whole plant.
*   C the rate of transpiration.
    D the height of the water in the tube.

89. _A_ Which transpirometer represents the normal control for the experiment?

90. _D_ In which would the rate of water loss be lowest?

91. _C_ Which tests the hypothesis that light is necessary for transpiration?

92. _B_ In which transpirometer would the rate of water loss be greatest?

93. A conclusion that could be drawn from this experiment is that

*   A leaves are a major factor in transpiration.
    B temperatures above 30°C increase transpiration rate.
    C photosynthetic rate influences transpiration.
    D sunlight is necessary for transpiration to occur.

The next five items refer to the following investigation.

Samples of five different plant parts were placed in five sealed containers of equal volume. The amount of carbon dioxide present in the containers at the beginning was 250 ml. After two days, it was as shown in the table. (Assume that experimental conditions not listed are identical in all five containers.)

CONTAINER	PLANT	PLANT PART	TEMPERATURE °C	CO_2 (in ml)
1	Myrtle	Leaf	15	100
2	Myrtle	Leaf	27	50
3	Myrtle	Stem	27	200
4	Oak	Root	27	300
5	Oak	Leaf	27	150

94. The experimental data indicate that oak leaves took up

    A more carbon dioxide at 27°C than at 15°C.
    B less carbon dioxide per day than did oak roots.
    C the same amount of carbon dioxide per day as did oak roots.
*   D more carbon dioxide per day than did oak roots.

95. How could you compare the amounts of carbon dioxide used per day at two different temperatures? Compare Containers

*   A 1 and 2.
    B 1 and 3.
    C 4 and 5.
    D 2 and 3.

96. In which container was photosynthesis taking place at the fastest rate?

    A 1
*   B 2
    C 3
    D 4

97. In which container was photosynthesis taking place at the slowest rate?

    A 2
*   B 3
    C 4
    D 5

98. In which container was photosynthesis *not* occurring?

    A 2
    B 3
*   C 4
    D 5

99. All of the stomates of a leaf were closed. Which of the following conditions could account for this?

    A Nighttime; plenty of water
*   B Daytime; little water
    C Daytime; guard cells full of water
    D Nighttime; guard cells full of water

100. Something in addition to atmospheric pressure is responsible for the rise of water in plant stems. Which of the following observations best indicates this?

*   A Plants grow to heights of 100 meters.
    B Plants will not grow unless supplied with water.
    C Plants continually carry on transpiration.
    D Tubules in plants' vascular systems have thick walls.

101. In plants growing in very hot, dry climates, photosynthesis is greatly reduced during the middle hours of the day. What is the best explanation for this?

    A No water is available for light reactions.
*   B Transpiration rate is very high. The stomates close and no carbon dioxide enters the leaves.
    C Enzymes of dark reactions are inactivated by high temperatures.
    D Wavelength of light is not suitable for photosynthesis.

102. For several centuries, people believed that a plant grew because its roots consumed soil. Which procedure would be most useful in testing this idea?

    A Find out if the same chemicals were present in plants and soil.

*   B See if the mass of soil in a pail decreases as a plant grows in the pail.

    C Note the mass of plants grown in several different types of soil.

    D Find out what effect wilting has on a plant's growth rate.

103. Later, people thought that all the matter in a plant came from water supplied to the plant. If this were true, which of the following would equal the gain in mass of a growing plant?

    A The mass of water poured on the plant

    B The difference between the masses of gases entering and leaving the plant

*   C The difference between the masses of water entering and leaving the plant

    D The sum of the masses of water and gases entering the plant.

21 Plant Growth and Reproduction

INFORMATION AND DEFINITIONS

1. Which of the following is necessary for seed germination?

    A Photosynthesis
* B Water absorption
    C Mineral absorption
    D Fertile soil

2. The energy for the early growth of seeds comes from

    A warm soil.
* B stored food.
    C light.
    D water.

3. The embryo of the seed is produced by growth of

    A mature pollen grains.
    B the fertilized fusion nucleus.
* C a zygote.
    D the endosperm.

4. The mature fruit is which part of the flower?

    A Style
    B Anther
* C Ovary
    D ~~Sepal~~ ovule

5. An example of a positive tropism would be the

    A upward growth of the shoot.
* B downward growth of the root.
    C lateral growth of the leaves.
    D downward movement of sugar.

6. In the flower, pollination is accomplished when

    A the sperm unites with the egg.
    B double fertilization occurs.
    C pollen is formed in the anther.
* D pollen is moved from anther to stigma.

7. The pollen-producing organ of a flower is composed of

    A stigma and style.
    B ovary and egg.
* C anther and filament.
    D sepal and petal.

8. Which of the following would be an example of vegetative propagation?

    A Cross-pollination
* B Grafting
    C Fertilization
    D Self-pollination

9. A seed and a spore differ in that

    A only the seed is a reproductive structure.
    B the spore is formed by a union of egg and sperm.
* C the seed is diploid; the spore is monoploid.
    D the spore produces a sporophyte; the seed produces a gametophyte.

10. In the life cycle of a flowering plant, the female gametophyte is a (an)

   A   plant that produces female flowers. *embryo sac containing*
 * B   small cluster of cells in the ovary of a flower.
   C   small, independent plant that is seldom seen.
   D   seed produced by fertilization.

11. The fertilized egg of vascular plants represents the

   A   first cell of the gametophyte generation.
   B   end of the gametophyte generation.
   C   end of the sporophyte generation.
 * D   first cell of the sporophyte generation.

12. A trend in development of higher plants is the decreasing

 * A   size of the gametophyte.
   B   photosynthetic rate.
   C   dominance of the sporophyte generation.
   D   importance of sexual reproduction.

13. Which of the following pairs of flower parts is directly involved with seed production?

   A   Sepals and petals
   B   Sepals and stamens
   C   Petals and pistils
 * D   Stamens and pistils

14. The small size of mosses probably is related to

   A   lack of cell walls.
   B   lack of a conducting system.
   C   small leaves.
   D   general lack of sex cells.

15. Organized conducting tissue is found in all green land plants except

   A   ferns and seed plants.
   B   mosses and ferns.
 * C   mosses and liverworts.
   D   ferns and flowering plants.

16. Auxins and gibberellins are found in plants. These chemicals are

   A   food for the embryo.
 * B   growth-controlling substances.
   C   carried by insects or by the wind.
   D   found only in land plants.

17. The embryo of a corn seed is to endosperm as the chick is to the

 * A   yolk.
   B   chorion.
   C   eggshell.
   D   sperm.

18. An animal is to its circulatory system as a plant is to its

   A   rhizome.
 * B   phloem.
   C   sporophyte.
   D   stem.

150

The next six items are based on the following table. The table shows the effects on germination of soaking four species of seeds.

Germination in the Dark (%)

PLANT	DAYS					
	2	4	6	8	10	12
1	75%	89%	-	-	-	-
2	37%	61%	79%	85%	-	-
3	12%	15%	17%	19%	21%	23%
4	0%	0%	0%	0%	0%	0%

Use the Key to evaluate the statements.

KEY A Supported by the evidence presented
    B Rejected by the evidence presented
    C Illogical, but not rejected by the evidence presented
    D Logical, but experiment does not test it

19. _D_ Species 3 seeds need more time for germination than do the other three species.

20. _A_ Species 3 seeds have a lower germination percentage in the dark than do Species 2 seeds.

21. _A_ Species 1 has the best germination capacity in the dark.

22. _D_ Species 4 may require light for germination.

23. _B_ Species 2 seeds need light for germination.

24. _B_ Soaking makes all four seed species germinate.

25. A seedling in a lightproof box is illuminated by a bright light from below. The shoot grows downward. Which of the following is true?

    A Positive geotropism is stronger than is positive phototropism.
*   B Positive phototropism is stronger than is negative geotropism.
    C Negative geotropism is stronger than is positive phototropism.
    D Negative phototropism is stronger than is positive geotropism.

The next six items refer to an experiment designed to test this hypothesis: Corn seeds do _not_ germinate at freezing temperatures.

Twenty corn grains were planted on moist paper in each of two petri dishes. The dishes were covered with black paper to keep out light. Dish 1 was kept at $0°C$; Dish 2 was kept at $25°C$.
    In Dish 2, 18 grains had germinated by Day 5. In Dish 1, no seeds had germinated by Day 10.

26. What is the variable in this experiment?

    A Light
    B Number of germinated seeds
*   C Temperature
    D Number of days

The following statements were suggested as conclusions based on this experiment. For these items, use the above information and the following Key.

KEY A Tentatively acceptable
    B Contrary to the data
    C Goes beyond the data
    D Probably correct but unrelated to this hypothesis

27. __B__ Corn grains will not germinate in darkness.

28. __A__ Corn grains do not germinate at freezing temperatures.

29. __D__ No growth occurs in mature corn plants at 0°C.

30. __D__ Moisture is necessary for the germination of corn grains.

31. __C__ The corn grains would have germinated more rapidly at 30°C than they did at 25°C.

For the next four items, refer to the following graphs, which show the results of an enperiment on germination of seeds.

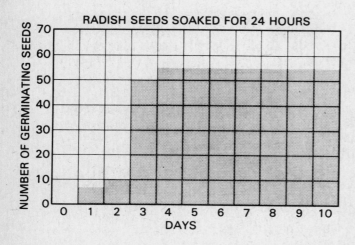

RADISH SEEDS SOAKED FOR 24 HOURS

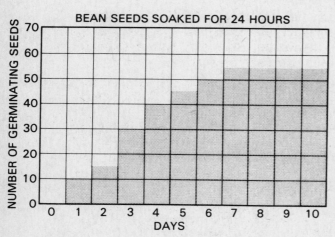

BEAN SEEDS SOAKED FOR 24 HOURS

32. A generalization can be made about the data. The generalization is that

   A 24 hours is the best soaking period for radish and bean seeds.
* B radish seeds germinate more rapidly than do bean seeds.
   C the bean seeds had a steady rate of germination.
   D most bean seeds of this kind require six days to germinate.

33. What would you say if someone asked you when most soaked radish seeds of this variety would germinate?

   A Two days after planting
   B One day after planting
* C Three days after planting
   D At least five days after planting

34. Which factor is the variable in this experiment?

   A Period of the soaking
   B Dishes in which seeds were planted
   C Rate of germination
* D Kind of seeds used

35. Suppose you were asked to test the hypothesis that atomic radiation slows down the rate of radish seed germination. Which of the following experimental designs would be the best one to use?

   A Use 25 radish seeds and 25 bean seeds and compare results.
   B Plant 50 irradiated seeds and note the effects of the radiation.
* C Plant 25 irradiated seeds and 25 normal seeds at the same time and compare results.
   D Plant 25 normal seeds and note results; then plant 25 irradiated seeds and compare results.

Seeds of three species of plants were treated with fungicide. In each of six large petri dishes, 50 seeds were placed on moist filter paper. They were kept at room temperature. The number of seeds germinating in each dish is recorded in the table.

SPECIES	IN LIGHT	IN DARK
X	42	7
Y	14	35
Z	35	37

The next five items are statements suggested as hypotheses being tested by this experiment. Classify each according to the Key.

KEY A Hypothesis being tested
     B Hypothesis *not* being tested
     C Not a hypothesis

36. C Some of the seeds in each dish germinated.

37. A Light is a factor that influences germination.

38. B Temperature is a factor that influences germination.

39. A The seeds of different plant species differ in germination requirements.

40. B The amount of moisture affects germination.

_____

The next ten items are based on the following information.

Certain desert annual plants have the ability to withstand drought. The reason for this lies in factors that control seed germination.

Question. How is germination regulated so that germination of these desert plants occurs?

Hypothesis 1. The amount of water available to the seed is the factor that controls germination.

Hypothesis 2. The required amount of water must come from a certain direction before seeds germinate.

Use the Key to classify the following observations about these plants.

KEY A Supports Hypothesis 1
     B Supports Hypothesis 2
     C Supports both hypotheses
     D Supports neither hypothesis

41. D Seeds do not germinate in soil of high salt content.

42. A Germination takes place only after at least 1.3 cm of rain has fallen in the desert.

43. D When 0.25 cm of rain falls, it leaves the upper 2.5 cm of soil as wet as 2.5 or 5 cm of rain.

44. B One year, 10.25 cm of rain fell in the desert, but no germination took place.

45. B The equivalent of 2.5 cm of rain was added from below the soil to soak the seeds in a container. No germination occurred.

46. Choose the best tentative conclusion based on the above observations.

*   A Something more than soaking is necessary for seed germination.
    B Soaking is all that is needed for seed germination.
    C Less water is needed for germination if water comes from above.
    D Desert conditions are more suitable for germination of desert plant seeds.

Additional Information. Assume that the direction from which water moves influences seed germination of desert plants.

Hypothesis 3. Something in the soil keeps seeds from germinating.

Hypothesis 4. Something on the seeds keeps them from germinating.

Use the following Key to classify the following observations.

KEY A Supports Hypothesis 3
     B Supports Hypothesis 4
     C Supports both hypotheses
     D Supports neither hypothesis

47. __A__ Some desert grass seeds germinate only after a high salt concentration in the soil has been washed away.

48. __D__ Seeds planted 61.5 cm deep in desert soil do not germinate.

49. __B__ Some desert seeds will germinate after bacterial action takes place on the seed surface.

50. __C__ Some desert seeds need several rains before germination occurs.

_____

The next 13 items are interpretations of data plotted on the following graph.

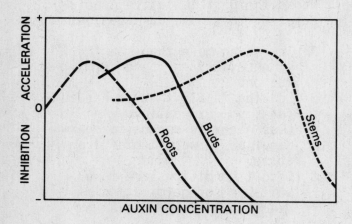

Use the Key to evaluate each statement.

KEY A Supported by the data
     B Contradicted by the data
     C Neither supported nor contradicted by the data

51. __C__ Buds produce more auxins than do either roots or stems.

52. __B__ Stems do not respond to auxins.

53. __A__ Roots react differently to auxins than do stems.

54. __B__ Plant roots do not respond to auxins.

55. __C__ Roots respond to different auxins than do stems.

56. __C__ Auxin excreted by roots protects the plant from disease.

57. __A__ Buds are inhibited by lower auxin concentrations than are stems.

58. __B__ Stem growth is always increased by the addition of auxins.

59. __A__ Root growth is stimulated by smaller amounts of auxins than is stem growth.

60. __C__ Root growth is inhibited by stem growth.

61. __C__ Bud growth is accelerated by stem growth.

62. __A__ High auxin concentrations will stunt plant growth.

63. __A__ There is a different optimum auxin concentration for growth acceleration in roots, buds, and stems.

_____

The next three items are based on the following experiment.

A biologist wanted to test the hypothesis that germinating seeds of two different species might influence one another. The biologist planted seeds of Species 1 (S1) and Species 2 (S2) in the same tray. The S1 seeds sprouted faster than did the S2 seeds.

64. The biologist decided to test the hypothesis that S2 seeds produce a substance that stimulates germination of S1 seeds. To do this, the biologist should

* A put an extract of germinating S2 seeds in a tray with germinating S1 seeds.
  B prepare several trays with varying numbers of S1 and S2 seeds.
  C prepare several trays each containing the same number of S1 and S2 seeds.
  D put an extract of germinating S1 seeds in a tray with germinating S2 seeds.

65. Suppose that Species 1 seeds might inhibit germination in Species 2 seeds. To test this hypothesis, the biologist should

  A put an extract of germinating S2 seeds in a tray with germinating S1 seeds.
  B plant several trays containing equal numbers of boiled S2 seeds and unboiled S1 seeds.
* C put an extract of germinating S1 seeds in a tray with germinating S2 seeds.
  D prepare several trays with varying numbers of S1 and S2 seeds.

66. In order for the results to be interpreted, the biologist also should germinate

  A S1 and S2 seeds in the dark.
* B S1 and S2 seeds in separate trays.
  C S1 and S2 seeds at various temperatures.
  D the same number of S1 seeds as S2 seeds.

The next six items relate to growth movements (tropisms) in plants. Using the Key below, identify each statement.

KEY A Positive geotropism
    B Negative geotropism
    C Positive phototropism
    D Negative phototropism
    E Neither geotropism nor phototropism

67. _A_ Roots of seeds germinating in the dark always grow downward.

68. _D_ Bermuda grass, strongly illuminated from the left, grows to the right.

69. _E_ If the path of a tree root's growth is obstructed by a rock, the root will grow around the rock.

70. _C_ In a lightproof box with a hole cut in it, plants will grow out through the hole.

71. _E_ When lightly touched, the leaves of a *Mimosa*, or sensitive plant, close.

72. _B_ Shoots of seeds germinated in the dark always grow upward.

The next three items are based on the following diagrams of plant life cycles.

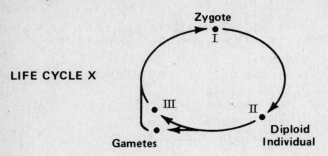

LIFE CYCLE X

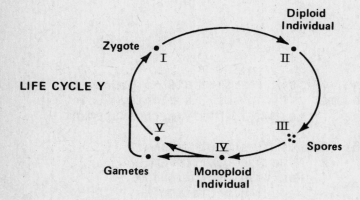

LIFE CYCLE Y

73. The cycle that most closely resembles the sexual life cycle of a moss plant is

    A X.
*   B Y.
    C all of Y except II.
    D all of Y except IV.

74. The stage in the life cycle of a fern that is recognized easily is represented by

    A I in X.
    B II in X.
    C IV in Y.
*   D II in Y.

75. Meiosis occurs between

    A I and II in X.
    B V and I in Y.
    C IV and V in Y.
*   D II and III in X.

76. Which of the following would *not* prevent self-pollination of a plant?

    A Cover the stamen
    B Cover the pistil
    C Remove the anther
*   D Remove the petals

77. The best assurance of cross-pollination of a flower species is

*   A production of stamen and pistils by two different plants.
    B flowers that are dull in color.
    C pollen that is not stickly.
    D a stamen that matures at the same time as does the pistil.

The next four items are based on the following information and diagram.

"A" represents a bean seedling that has been marked into four zones. (Zone I is the root cap.) "B" is the same seedling after three days' growth.

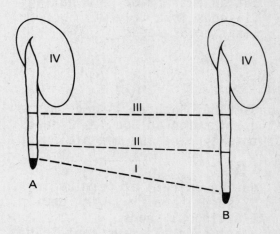

78. The zone of active cell elongation is

    A I.
*   B II.
    C III.
    D IV.

79. The greatest amount of stored food is in Zone

    A I.
    B II.
    C III.
* D IV.

80. The zone of the root where cells are differentiating is

    A I.
    B II.
* C III.
    D IV.

81. If the seedling were placed on its side, auxin would cause the root to grow downward. The effect of auxin would be greatest in Zone

    A I.
* B II.
    C III.
    D IV.

The next three items are based on the following diagrams.

START

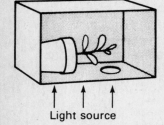

Light source

ONE WEEK

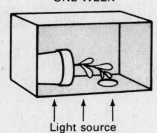

Light source

82. The stem tip grows downward. The best explanation for this is that, in the stem,

    A positive geotropism is stronger than negative geotropism.
* B positive phototropism is stronger than negative geotropism.
    C negative geotropism is stronger than positive phototropism.
    D negative phototropism is stronger than positive geotropism.

83. After one week, the roots of the plant would appear to be growing

    A upward.
* B downward.
    C toward the bottom of the pot.
    D equally in all directions.

84. The root-growth response would be classed as

    A positive phototropism.
    B negative phototropism.
* C positive geotropism.
    D negative geotropism.

22 Animal Behavior

INFORMATION AND DEFINITIONS

1. A boy walks through the woods and a rabbit runs away from him. He says "that rabbit is running because it doesn't like me." This is an example of

    A perception.
*   B anthropomorphism.
    C conditioning.
    D tropism.

2. Birds of a given species usually build nests in an area at widely spaced intervals. This is an example of

    A learning.
    B imprinting.
    C migration.
*   D territoriality.

7. Most fish orient their dorsal (top) surface toward light. This is an example of

    A reasoning.
    B imprinting.
*   C a taxis.
    D a learned behavior.

4. Many behaviors seem independent of an organism's past experiences. These behaviors are

*   A innate.
    B conditioned.
    C trial-and-error.
    D learned.

5. The most predictable and simplest behaviors are

*   A taxes and reflexes.
    B learning and reasoning.
    C habituation patterns.
    D conditioned responses.

6. Imprinting is characterized by

    A a slow decline in learning after training.
*   B brief exposure at an early age and long-lasting results.
    C few errors in a maze after only a few trials.
    D gradual training that produces a response to another stimulus.

7. The statement, "Prairie dogs dig burrows in which to raise their young," is an example of

    A imprinting.
    B learning.
    C ethology.
    D teleology.

8. Mature male horses often are more aggressive than adult female horses, even though both groups were equally gentle when young. This change probably occurs because of changes in the

    A environment.
*   B endocrine system.
    C external stimuli.
    D circadian rhythms.

9. Salmon swimming upriver to spawn are exhibiting which of the following kinds of behavior?

    A Imprinting
    B Territoriality
*   C Migration
    D Habituation

10. Which of the following probably is *not* a kind of learned behavior?

    A Conditioning
    B Habituation
    C Imprinting
*   D Migration

11. People who fly across several time zones in a few hours experience "jet lag" at their destinations. "Jet lag" is an upset in a person's

    A perception.
    B pheromones.
    C conditioning.
*   D circadian rhythm.

12. Circadian rhythms are

    A not related to external stimuli.
    B not related to survival.
    C times of maximum alertness.
*   D related to cycles of light and dark.

13. Which of the following mistakes occurs most commonly in the study of animal behavior?

    A Misinterpreting which animals are male and which are female
*   B Assuming that other animals perceive stimuli as humans do
    C Not collecting enough data
    D Not classifying animals correctly

APPLICATION AND INQUIRY

For the next three items, refer to the following data and graph.

Three groups of hamsters were tested daily in a maze. The route through the maze forked ten times and none of the choices could be repeated. The number of errors of choice was counted for each hamster and an average was calculated for each group.

    One of the groups received no food reward, one received a regular food reward, and one received no food reward until the fourth day.

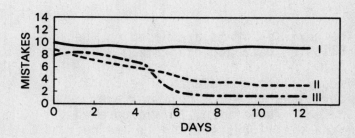

14. <u>I</u> Which group did not receive a food reward?

15. <u>III</u> Which group did not receive a food reward until the fourth day?

16. __II__ Which group received regular food rewards?

_____

Use the following Key to classify the next six statements.

KEY A Conclusion based on experimental results
     B Statement contrary to the results
     C Statement is unrelated to or goes beyond the data.

17. __A__ Almost no learning took place unless rewards were given.

18. __C__ The hamsters of Group III learned the maze quickly because they reacted negatively to a shock stimulus.

19. __A__ The number of errors made by Group III decreased greatly when a food reward was given.

20. __A__ Hamsters have the ability to learn a complex maze within a week.

21. __C__ At the end of Day 15, hamsters who had received food rewards made no errors.

22. __B__ Learning takes place faster when rewards follow an initial unrewarded period.

_____

The next six items are based on the following data and diagrams.

Twenty flies are placed in each of four glass tubes. The tubes are sealed. Tubes I and II are covered with foil; Tubes III and IV are not covered. The tubes are placed as shown. Then they are exposed to red light for five minutes. The number of flies in the uncovered part of each tube is shown in the drawing.

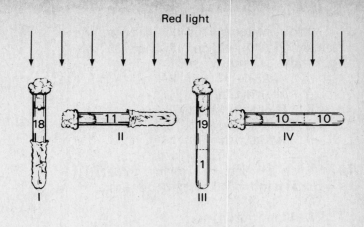

Red light

23. This experiment shows that flies respond to

     A red light but not to gravity.
*   B gravity but not to red light.
     C both red light and gravity.
     D neither red light nor gravity.

In a second experiment, blue light was used instead of red. The results are shown in the drawing.

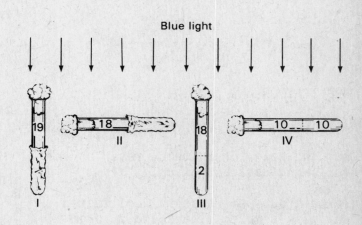

Blue light

24. These data show that flies respond to

     A blue light but not to gravity.
     B gravity but not to blue light.
*   C both blue light and gravity.
     D neither blue light nor gravity.

25. From both experiments, one can conclude that flies react to

    A red light but not to blue light.
*   B blue light but not to red light.
    C both blue and red light.
    D neither blue nor red light.

26. Which tubes served as controls for the light variable?

    A I and II
    B II and III
*   C III and IV
    D IV and I

27. Which tubes served as controls for the gravity variable?

*   A II and IV
    B II and III
    C III and IV
    D V and I

28. These experiments tested the flies' responses to

    A red light only.
    B blue light only.
    C gravity and blue light only.
*   D red and blue light and gravity.

The next nine items are based on a study of the dispersal tendency of herring gulls. The gulls were tagged when they hatched. The data in the chart are based on the recapture of the gulls. The chart shows the ages of the birds. It also shows the distance from the place of hatching to where each bird was recaptured.

Use the following Key to classify the items.

KEY A Justified by the data
       B Contrary to the data
       C Insufficient information to evaluate the statement

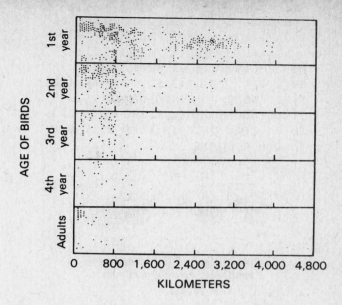

29. __B__ Adult birds fly 1,600 km from the nesting site.

30. __A__ Young birds tend to leave the areas where they hatched.

31. __C__ Young birds are at a competitive disadvantage with older birds that have established territories.

32. __C__ The first-year gulls mated and established nesting sites 2,400 km from where they were hatched.

33. __A__ Most of the recaptured birds were one-year-old birds.

34. __C__ Dispersal tendency in young birds relieves population pressure where they hatched.

35. __C__ Those birds that fly farthest from home are all dead by the fifth year.

36. __C__ Usually, only female birds fly farther than 1,600 km from the hatching site.

37. __B__ The greatest dispersal tendency is found among three-year-old birds.

The next nine items are based on the following information.

Fermenting grapes were placed in each of five plates. Twenty fruit flies were released 6 meters away. After 30 seconds, flies were clustered around the plates as shown in the diagram.

I
Clear glass
open top

II
Clear glass
sealed shut

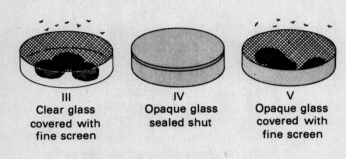

III
Clear glass
covered with
fine screen

IV
Opaque glass
sealed shut

V
Opaque glass
covered with
fine screen

Use the Key to classify the next six items.

KEY A Acceptable hypothesis based on the data
     B Unacceptable hypothesis based on the data
     C Reasonable hypothesis but not based on the data
     D Unacceptable because of anthropomorphism or teleology

38. __D__ The flies were hungry. The smell of grapes meant food, so they flew to the grapes to satisfy their hunger.

39. __A__ The flies responded positively to the odor of fermenting grapes.

40. __D__ The flies knew they could not get food, because they could not see the grapes in Plate IV.

41. __B__ The flies responded to a visual stimulus.

42. __C__ Movement of the flies was random between plates until they encountered Plate I where they were able to feed.

43. __A__ Flies may not be able to see through glass.

Use the following additional data to respond to the next items.

After ten minutes, the following numbers of flies were found at the plates.

Plate I   17
Plate II   0
Plate III   2
Plate IV   0
Plate V   1

44. The additional information indicates which of the following types of behavior?

    A Taxis
    B Migration
    C Conditioning
*   D Trial-and-error learning

45. The most probable stimulus for this behavior was

    A purple light reflected by the purple grapes.
*   B some chemical from the fermenting grapes.
    C the clear glass of Plates I and III.
    D the sight of the grapes.

46. The results could be explained in terms of

    A negative chemotaxis.
*   B positive chemotaxis.
    C negative phototaxis.
    D positive phototaxis.

The next 13 items refer to the italicized parts of the following paragraphs. Each part in italics is an item. Identify each item with a response from the Key. Read all paragraphs before responding to the items.

KEY A Problem (stated or implied)
    B Hypothesis (possible solution to problem)
    C Observation or result of experiment
    D Question

(47) *Some animals have the ability to change color.* (48) *How they accomplish this has long been a mystery.* (49) *When a catfish is placed in an aquarium that has a black bottom and sides, the fish becomes black in a few days.* (50) *When the same fish is transferred to a tank that has a white bottom and sides, it becomes very pale, almost white.* (51) *Could it have some type of color receptor in its skin?* (52) *Or is the sense receptor that is responsible for this located in the eyes?*

If the sensitivity were due to stimulation of the eyes, (53) *blinding should inhibit the ability to change color.* (54) *Blinded fish were unable to respond to changes in the background color,* but light intensity does not seem to be the whole answer.

If light intensity were the only stimulus, (55) *fish in a dark tank under bright light would become lighter, and fish in a white tank under dim light would become darker.* This would happen because more light would be reflected from a brightly lighted, dark tank than from a dimly lighted white one.

But this was not the case. (56) *The fish turned white even in a very dimly lighted, white tank. They turned dark in a brightly illuminated, dark one.*

In the next phase of the experiment, the amount of direct light and reflected light was varied. This experiment showed (57) *that the darkness of the fish was proportional to the ratio of direct light to reflected light.*

This suggested that (58) *more than one receptor was involved in the mechanism of adjustment.* Glass lenses were fitted over the fish's eyes. (59) *When the lower half of each lens was blackened, shielding the eyes from the bottom and walls of the tank, the fish became dark even on a white background. If the upper half were blackened, concealing direct light, the fish became pale even when placed in a black aquarium.*

Answers:

47	C	54	C
48	A	55	B
49	C	56	C
50	C	57	C
51	D	58	B
52	D	59	C
53	B		

The next eight items refer to the following information and graphs.

A group of scientists were working with butterflies. They presented the males with different kinds of paper "female butterflies" attached to the end of a fishing line. They used many of these models. In each model, one characteristic was changed. The results are shown in the graphs.

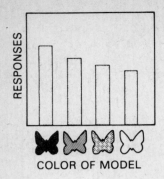 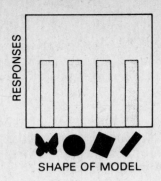

RESPONSES

COLOR OF MODEL

SHAPE OF MODEL

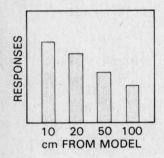 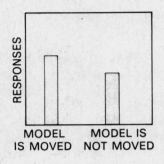

RESPONSES

10 20 50 100
cm FROM MODEL

RESPONSES

MODEL IS MOVED | MODEL IS NOT MOVED

Use the Key to classify the statements below.

KEY A Justified by the data
B Contrary to the data
C Insufficient evidence to evaluate the statement

60. __C__ The males could not see the models if they were more than 100 cm away.

61. __B__ Of the factors studied, the males responded to only one anatomical clue.

62. __C__ The sense of smell is important in the male's detection of the female.

63. __A__ Males responded to many different colors.

64. __A__ Movement of the model was a significant factor in attracting the male.

65. __B__ The shape of the model was a significant factor.

66. __B__ The farther away the model, the greater was the response.

67. The combination of characteristics most likely to cause a response in a male is

    A shape and distance only.
    B distance and color only.
    C shape, color, and movement.
* D color, movement, and distance.
_____

Certain parts of the following paragraphs are in italics. Each italicized part is an item. Read the paragraphs before answering the next eight items. Use the following Key.

KEY A Problem (stated or implied)
B Hypothesis (possible solution to problem)
C Statement of observations
D A prediction

(68) *Every few years, large groups of lemmings (small rodents) march for many kilometers.* They scarcely stop to eat or rest. They eventually plunge into lakes, rivers, and fjords, where they drown. (69) *What causes lemmings to do this has long been a mystery.*

This behavior has been explained (70) *as a result of the population reaching the limit of the food supply.* But (71) *these mass movements often occur in years when there is no food shortage.* (72) *In Sweden in 1963, hordes of lemmings moved south.* (73) *At a certain road in their path, 44 of them crossed per minute.* Although there was plenty of food available, when one of the lemmings died, it was eaten by the others. Contrary to what one might expect, these marching lemmings are healthy, mature young born the previous spring.

About every ten years, the snowshoe hares of North America die of unknown causes. Examination of the corpses shows (74) *they are neither undernourished nor diseased.* However, they suddenly go into convulsions and die.

Meadow voles of New York State show almost identical behavior. (75) *Is it possible that increased social disorganization causes a fatal state of physical exhaustion?*

Answers:

68	C	72	C
69	A	73	C
70	B	74	C
71	C	75	B

For the next seven items, use the Key to classify behaviors found in a variety of organisms.

KEY A Innate behavior
     B Trial-and-error learning
     C Conditioning
     D Reasoning

76. __C__ A toad catches robber flies. When presented with a bumblebee, about the same size as a robber fly, the toad caught it and was stung. The toad no longer catches robber flies.

77. __B__ Cockroaches can learn a maze if food is provided at the end of the maze.

78. __A__ Certain ants carry pieces of leaves into their burrows where fungi can grow safely and be used by the ants for food.

79. __D__ A chimpanzee climbs a ladder, pulls a hanging tray by a cord, gets onto the tray, and swings to a ledge where there is food.

80. __A__ Certain species of birds build intricate nests.

81. __A__ A young monkey clings to an inanimate object that is warm, soft, and provides milk.

82. __C__ A tropical fish owner taps on the aquarium every time he feeds the fish. The fish then come to the top for food. One day a friend visited and tapped on the aquarium while looking at the fish. The fish came to the surface.

83. Which of the following is an example of an inherited behavior pattern?

    A A rat finds its way through a maze.
*   B A tropical fish chases another fish away from its nest.
    C A monkey opens a cage and gets a banana
    D A newly hatched duck follows a model resembling a female quail.

84. You are asked to determine whether a certain behavior pattern is inherited. The best experimental procedure would be to isolate newborn animals and

*   A see whether they develop the behavior.
    B observe their behavior when placed with others of their species after weeks of isolation.
    C condition them to behave in the desired manner.
    D allow them to observe the behavior of others of their species without association.

85. Golden plovers migrate between Canada and South America each year. Young birds hatched in Canada make the trip to South America unescorted by older birds. This flight of the young is an example of

    A imprinting.
    B territoriality.
*   C innate behavior.
    D memory and reasoning.

_____

The next three items are based on experiments with European chaffinches.

86. Finches raised in isolation can give *calls* characteristic of their species, but they cannot sing a complete and normal *song*. This information suggests that

*   A the call is inherited and the song is learned.
    B the song is inherited and the call is learned.
    C both the call and the song are inherited.
    D both the call and the song are learned.

87. Finches raised in isolation and allowed to hear a recording of the song of their own species learn the song properly. But if they hear a recording of a similar song of a different species, they do not learn the song. These findings suggest that

    A finches have a limited ability to learn.
    B song-learning under laboratory conditions is different from learning in the wild.
*   C recognition of the song is inherited.
    D raising finches in isolation impairs their ability to learn.

88. Taken together, the results reported above suggest that

    A the song is learned not inherited.
    B the song is inherited not learned.
    C the song is neither learned nor inherited.
*   D the song is both inherited and learned.

_____

INFORMATION AND DEFINITIONS

1. The major limiting factor for green plants in the open ocean is

    A depth.
* B light.
    C temperature.
    D current.

2. The factors limiting growth in a tropical rain forest are

    A temperature and light.
* B growing space and light.
    C temperature and length of growing season.
    D rainfall and length of growing season.

3. The ecosystem that can support the fewest species of animals is the

    A coniferous forest.
    B deciduous forest.
    C tropical rain forest.
* D tundra.

The next ten items relate to the principal forests of the world. Use the Key to classify the items.

KEY A Coniferous forest
      B Temperate deciduous forest
      C Tropical rain forest

4. _A_ The vegetation is a forest of spruce, fir, and pine.

5. _A_ The forest has the lowest average temperature.

6. _A_ Deer, moose, and beaver are the most plentiful mammals.

7. _B_ A definite shrub layer grows under the trees.

8. _C_ Many of its trees produce fleshy, edible fruits.

9. _C_ The forest has the greatest annual rainfall.

10. _C_ The forest receives the most radiant energy per year.

11. _B_ Oak and maple are typical trees in the forest.

12. _C_ The climate is very warm and unchanging.

13. _B_ Most of the trees shed their leaves in the winter.

---

14. Which of the following sets of terrestrial environments is arranged in series from most rainfall to least?

    A Tundra, coniferous forest, grassland
    B Rain forest, desert, deciduous forest
    C Coniferous forest, tundra, rain forest
*   D Deciduous forest, coniferous forest, desert

15. Successful populations of evergreen trees, red squirrels, moose, snowshoe hares, and beavers would be part of ecosystems in the

* A coniferous forest.
  B tundra.
  C deciduous forest.
  D tropical rain forest.

16. In the tundra regions, you would expect to find

  A many producer species.
* B few species of plants and animals.
  C many mammalian species.
  D many omnivores.

17. The phrase, "three blackberry bushes per square meter," is a description of

  A dispersal.
  B abundance.
* C density.
  D propagation.

18. An ecosystem cannot exist without

* A producers.
  B secondary consumers.
  C carnivores.
  D omnivores.

19. An ecosystem is defined best as

  A animals in their habitats.
  B plant producers and animal consumers.
  C plants, animals, and microorganisms.
* D interactions of organisms and environment.

20. Some organisms can live on the vertical face of a rock that is exposed to the ocean at the tidal zone. These organisms are distributed according to their adaptations for increasing resistance to

  A temperature change.
* B drying out.
  C oxygen deficiency.
  D changes in salt concentration.

21. The biosphere includes

  A plants and animals only.
  B nonliving material only.
* C both living and nonliving material.
  D all environments except those that are too harsh to support life.

APPLICATION AND INQUIRY

The next seven items are based on the following diagram of a forest. Use the letters on the left to answer the first five items.

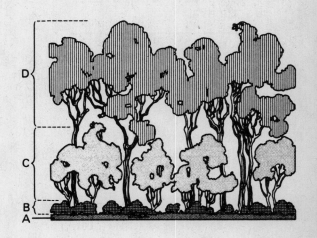

22. __D__ Where is most of the photo-synthesis occurring?

23. __B__ A slight decrease in light would be most critical for the plants in which layer?

24. __B__ Where would most annual herbs be found?

25. __A__ Where would the humidity be the greatest?

26. __A__ Where would the most decom-posers be found?

27. If the trees shown are deciduous, then this type of ecosystem most likely would be found in

* A eastern United States.
  B Central America.
  C western United States.
  D central Canada.

28. If this forest were located in Central America or southern Florida, it probably would be a

  A coniferous rain forest.
  B mountain coniferous forest.
* C tropical rain forest.
  D temperate deciduous forest.

The next eight items relate to some of the earth's major ecosystems. Use the Key to classify the items.

KEY A Tundra
    B Desert
    C Grassland

29. __B__ Evaporation rate is highest.

30. __C__ Most of the animals found are hoofed.

31. __A__ Area can support lichens, mosses, and tiny flowering plants, but no large trees.

32. __B__ This ecosystem has very low amounts of precipitation.

33. __B__ This ecosystem has the high-est average temperature.

34. __B__ In this ecosystem, the plants have very widespread roots.

35. __A__ Summers provide only a month or two of favorable weather.

36. __B__ Most of the trees and shrubs shed their leaves in the summer.

The next 11 items relate to data plotted on the graph. The graph shows the numbers of plant and animal plankton in a relatively deep lake in northern United States.

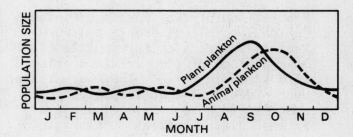

Use the Key to classify the following interpretations.

KEY A Reasonable interpretation of the data
    B Contradicted by the data
    C More data needed to make an interpretation
    D Restatement of the data

37. __C__ The number of plant plankton is directly correlated to light intensity.

38. __D__ There is a seasonal change in the amount of plant plankton.

39. _C_ The lake is located in upper New York State.

40. _B_ The lowest level of change in number of animal plankton is in the summer.

41. _D_ The peak (top of the curve) for animal plankton is lower than the peak for plant plankton.

42. _D_ The cause of decreased plant plankton probably is a drop in water temperature.

43. _D_ The greatest increase of plant plankton occurred during the summer.

44. _B_ There are no animal plankton in this lake during the winter.

45. _A_ The growth of animal plankton is related to the growth of the plant plankton.

46. _C_ Some of the plant plankton are larger than the animal plankton.

47. _A_ The plant plankton serve as the producers for the animal plankton.

The next seven items refer to the following information and investigations.

Populations of two species of insects (which look almost identical) were kept in separate culture bottles for long periods of time. Both species were adequately fed. They were reared under identical conditions. Each species had a high rate of survival in the culture bottles. This rate continued even when the temperature and humidity were varied.

As a further investigation, new culture bottles were prepared and kept under the conditions indicated in the diagram. A male and a female of each species were placed in each bottle. The percentage of individuals of each species present in each bottle after six months is recorded below.

% OF INDIVIDUALS AFTER 6 MONTHS		CULTURE 1	CULTURE 2	CULTURE 3	CULTURE 4	CULTURE 5	CULTURE 6
	Species X	100%	10%	75%	15%	40%	0%
	Species Y	0%	90%	25%	85%	60%	100%
CONDITIONS	Temperature °C	30°C	30°C	22°C	22°C	15°C	15°C
	Relative Humidity	80%	20%	80%	20%	80%	20%

Use the following Key.

KEY A Species X
     B Species Y
     C Both species
     D Not enough information to
        make the decision

48. _D_ Which species would you
        expect to find on the bare
        ground where summer temper-
        atures exceed 85°C?

49. _B_ Which species would you
        expect to find in a dry
        habitat?

50. _A_ Which species would you
        expect to find under vegeta-
        tion in mid-summer?

51. _D_ Which species would survive
        extremely cold winters?

52. _B_ Which species is best suited
        to desert conditions?

53. _C_ Which species would you
        expect to find under vegeta-
        tion in the early spring?

54. _A_ Which species is best suited
        to living in a tropical rain
        forest?

_____

171

24 Interactions in Ecosystems

1. Knowledge of the cycles of elements in ecosystems helps us to understand

    A that all organisms need nitro-gen and fresh water to live.
    B that these cycles operate all the time.
*   C how matter circulates through living systems.
    D why bacteria form nitrogen compounds.

2. In a community, matter and energy are

    A similar, because both flow through the system.
    B similar, because both cycle within the system.
*   C different, because matter cycles and energy flows.
    D different, because energy cycles and matter flows.

3. Which of these describes a path-way of energy through the living system?

*   A Light energy $\longrightarrow$ chemical energy $\longrightarrow$ heat
    B Light energy $\longrightarrow$ heat $\longrightarrow$ chemical energy
    C Heat $\longrightarrow$ light energy $\longrightarrow$ chemical energy
    D Chemical energy $\longrightarrow$ heat $\longrightarrow$ light energy

4. An example of the primary consumers in a community are the

    A bacteria that live in the soil.
    B cats that eat moles.
*   C rabbits that eat leaves and stems.
    D fleas that bite dogs and cats.

5. Life on earth would disappear if all the

    A decomposers disappeared.
*   B producers disappeared.
    C primary consumers disappeared.
    D secondary consumers disappeared.

6. There are always fewer organisms at each higher step of the food pyramid because

    A each organism is larger than the previous one.
*   B energy is lost as heat in each step of the pyramid.
    C at each step, the reproduc-tive rate decreases.
    D more organisms die at each higher level of the food chain.

_____

Use this Key for the next ten items.

KEY A Primary consumers
      B Secondary consumers
      C Producers
      D Decomposers

7. _C_ These organisms capture energy in photosynthesis.

8. _C_ These are the organisms in a food web most likely to increase in number first.

9. _A_ These organisms collect and convert carbohydrates to protein.

10. _A_ Mice eat grass.

11. _B_ Hawks eat mice.

12. _B_ Mosquitoes bite cows.

13. _D_ These organisms digest dead plant and animal tissues.

14. _C_ Carbon is made available to most organisms by the activities of these organisms.

15. _C_ These organisms change light energy to chemical energy.

16. _D_ Most of these organisms are microscopic.

_____

17. Which of the following statements describes best the work done by decomposers?

*   A They release carbon from dead bodies as carbon dioxide.
     B They provide calcium for plants by taking it from soil or water.
     C They create new sources of oxygen and release free nitrogen.
     D They prevent the escape of energy from organisms to the environment.

18. Which best represents the flow of energy in a food chain?

    A Sparrow⟶seeds⟶hawk⟶bacteria
    B Hawk⟶seeds⟶bacteria⟶sparrow
* C Seeds⟶sparrow⟶hawk⟶bacteria
    D Sparrow⟶hawk⟶bacteria⟶seeds

19. Which organisms are most necessary for the survival of primary consumers?

*   A Producers
     B Decomposers
     C Secondary consumers
     D Nitrogen-fixing bacteria

20. A steady state would be most characteristic of a community in which succession

    A is repeatedly disrupted.
    B is occurring slowly.
    C is occurring rapidly.
* D has ended.
      _____

The next seven items are concerned with the fact that organisms can be divided into producers and consumers. Use the Key to classify the statements.

KEY A Producers only
      B Consumers only
      C Both consumers and producers
      D Neither consumers nor producers

21. _A_ Convert light energy into chemical energy

22. _C_ Supply food for consumers

23. _A_ Use the energy of sunlight in the manufacture of food

24. _D_ Have the ability to create energy

25. _B_ Are unable to make their own
         food

26. _C_ Have the ability to store
         energy in chemical bonds

27. _C_ Depend on organic molecules
         for food
         _____

28. An area receives large amounts of
rainfall but it supports only desert-
like vegetation. This probably is
an area of high

    A altitude.
    B density.
*   C runoff.
    D temperature.

29. A mushroom growing on a rotting
tree is a

    A producer.
    B primary consumer.
    C secondary consumer.
*   D decomposer.

30. Nitrates are to bacteria as
oxygen is to

    A animals.
*   B green plants.
    C consumers.
    D decomposers.

31. Which of the following ecosystems
has the lowest productivity?

*   A Tundra
    B Coniferous forest
    C Deciduous forest
    D Tropical rain forest

32. The greater the number of path-
ways in a food web,

    A the greater is the energy flow
       through the ecosystem.
*   B the greater is the stability
       of the ecosystem.
    C the larger is the population
       of producers.
    D the larger is the population
       of consumers.

APPLICATION AND INQUIRY

33. An outcome of the activities of
bacteria and mushrooms is to

    A return energy to the air.
*   B release elements from dead
       organisms.
    C decrease heat in the system.
    D decrease the supply of
       elements.

34. If carbon dioxide (CO_2) were with-
drawn from the biosphere, which organisms would first experience
negative biological effects?

    A Primary consumers
*   B Producers
    C Secondary consumers
    D Decomposers

35. A farmer starts a colony of rats
and a colony of mink. He feeds some
of the rats to the mink. He then
feeds some of the mink to the remaining rats. By feeding the rats to
the mink and the mink to the rats,
the farmer hopes to get mink skins
for nothing. Is this possible?

    A Yes, because the system would
       be in a steady state.
    B Yes, because energy lost in
       one organism is gained back
       in the other.
    C No, because this would make
       both organisms secondary
       consumers.
*   D No, because lost energy is
       not replaced.

36. It is easily seen that nonproducers are dependent on producers and other consumers. We can say, however, that producers are dependent on other organisms because

    A they are green.
    B they obtain energy to produce cellular materials from the sun.
*   C they depend on decomposers for essential compounds such as nitrates.
    D their energy is made from minerals in the soil.

37. A volcano rises from the floor of the ocean. The resulting island gradually becomes populated with living organisms. The most likely order of colonization is

*   A blue-green algae, grass, trees, birds, snakes.
    B birds, snakes, trees, blue-green algae, grass.
    C snakes, birds, trees, blue-green algae, grass.
    D trees, grass, birds, snakes, blue-green algae.

The next 12 items refer to the forests of the Pacific Northwest. Douglas firs, cedars, and hemlocks are the principal trees of the region. Characteristics of each are listed in the table.

CHARACTERISTICS	
DOUGLAS FIR	CEDAR AND HEMLOCK
Seedlings die in shade.	Seedlings grow in shade.
Seedlings grow well on ashes.	Seedlings do not grow well on ashes.
Seeds are winged.	Seeds are not winged.

38. When an old Douglas fir tree dies in a dense forest, its place will be taken by

    A Douglas fir seedlings only.
    B cedar seedlings only.
*   C a mixture of cedars and hemlocks.
    D hemlock seedlings only.

39. The effect of a fire in this area should be to increase the number of

*   A Douglas firs.
    B cedars.
    C hemlocks.
    D pines.

Classify the next items using the Key.

KEY A Observation
      B Inference
      C Hypothesis
      D False statement

40. D The normal climax of a Douglas fir, cedar, and hemlock community should be a Douglas fir forest.

41. A The seeds of the Douglas fir are winged.

42. C After a fire in this community, the Douglas fir seedlings will enter, grow well, and crowd out other seedlings.

43. B The young Douglas fir trees do not grow in mature Douglas fir forests.

44. C If there are no fires in the forests, the Douglas firs will disappear when the present trees die out.

45. D Openings that allow the growth of cedars and hemlocks are created by fires.

46. __B__ In order to maintain the Douglas fir forests, complete logging of small areas is necessary, followed by burning of stumps and clearing.

47. __B__ Fire is necessary for the maintenance of some forests.

48. __A__ Cedars and hemlocks grow well in shade.

49. __B__ The stands of trees in a Douglas fir forest are all about the same size.

_____

The next seven items refer to the following diagram.

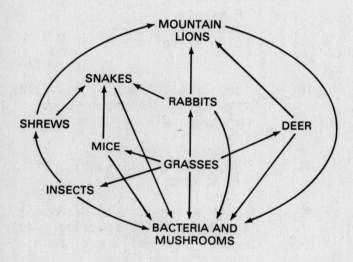

50. The diagram illustrates a

    A food chain.
*   B food web.
    C succession.
    D water cycle.

51. Which are primary consumers?

    A Mountain lions
*   B Deer
    C Grasses
    D Snakes

52. Which are decomposers?

    A Grasses
    B Shrews
*   C Mushrooms
    D Mountain lions

53. Which are the most important in supplying energy for the organisms in the diagram?

*   A Grasses
    B Mice
    C Bacteria
    D Shrews

54. The only producers shown here are

*   A grasses.
    B mushrooms.
    C mice.
    D deer.

55. The total mass of all the individuals in which group would be the greatest?

    A Shrews
    B Bacteria
    C Rabbits
*   D Grasses

56. The sequence, grass⟶insect⟶ shrew⟶mountain lion, represents a

    A niche.
    B food web.
    C carbon cycle.
*   D food chain.

_____

The next eight items concern the similarities and differences between matter and energy. Use the Key to classify the items.

KEY A Matter only
      B Energy only
      C Both matter and energy
      D Neither matter nor energy

57. _A_ Includes molecules that move in cycles from abiotic to biotic and back to abiotic factors

58. _D_ Moves from abiotic factors to biotic factors and stops

59. _C_ Can be changed from one form to another by the activities of organisms

60. _C_ Can be passed from one organism to another

61. _B_ Is constantly being lost from the ecosystem

62. _C_ Present in organic compounds

63. _B_ Is returned from biotic part of an ecosystem to the abiotic part as heat

64. _C_ The total quantity returned to the abiotic part from the biotic part equals the amount provided by the abiotic to the biotic.

———————————

Deerflies lay their eggs on grass. A grazing deer inhales some of these eggs. The eggs cling to the membranes of the deer's nose and hatch into wormlike forms called maggots. Because these maggots feed on material in the deer's head, the deer soon dies.

65. The deer is a

    A producer.
*   B primary consumer.
    C secondary consumer.
    D decomposer.

66. The deerfly maggots are

    A producers.
    B primary consumers.
*   C secondary consumers.
    D decomposers.

67. The grass-deer-maggot relationship represents a(an)

    A energy pyramid.
*   B food chain.
    C carbon cycle.
    D food web.

———————————

The next five items refer to a hypothetical study of a region in the southern United States. The area supported populations of deer and wolves. In 1915, a program was started to protect the deer by eliminating the wolves. By 1925, the wolves had been completely removed, and the deer population had increased to 100,000. By 1940, the deer population had dropped to 10,000 sick, weak, and starved individuals. These data are plotted in the graph.

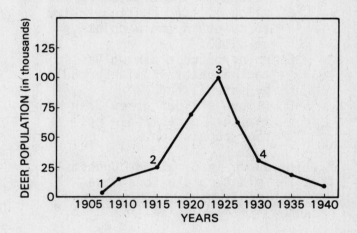

68. In what year was the deer population at its lowest point?

*   A 1907
    B 1924
    C 1930
    D 1940

69. The slope of the line from 2 to 3 indicates

*   A great change.
    B small change.
    C uneven change.
    D no change.

70. The wolves played an important part in the life of the deer. They were important because they

    A competed with the deer and thus kept the numbers of both species down.
    B ate only healthy deer.
* C kept the deer population down to a point where there was enough food available.
    D increased competition among the deer for available food.

By 1927, some people were aware that something should be done to correct the situation.

71. The best long-range solution to the problem would have been to

    A allow unlimited hunting to reduce the population.
    B allow limited hunting to try to maintain the population at 4,000.
* C reintroduce a few wolves so that a natural balance could be established.
    D remove all but a few deer and let them establish a new deer population.

72. The above information suggests that the plant populations were reduced. This would have happened because

    A the weather had been dry for several years causing a drought.
    B the soil was not properly fertilized by the animal wastes and decayed remains of the wolves.
* C the large deer population had eaten all the plants with food value.
    D hunters and tourists over-used the area, destroying the vegetation.

The next 11 items are based on the following information.

In temperate areas, mountain slopes facing south receive more direct sunlight than slopes facing north. As a result, the south-facing slopes are hotter and drier.

Use the Key to identify the statements, which are inferences about north- and south-facing slopes.

KEY A North-facing slopes only
      B South-facing slopes only
      C Both slopes
      D Neither slope

73. B After a storm, snow melts faster on these slopes.

74. A Snow accumulation usually is greater on these slopes.

75. B In early spring, these slopes are the first to provide food for primary consumers.

76. B There is much open space on these slopes.

77. C These slopes support a food web of primary and higher-level consumers.

78. A Vegetation on these slopes is lush.

79. B Drought-tolerant grasses often are abundant on these slopes.

80. D Decomposers are absent from the food webs on these slopes.

81. A Shade-tolerant flowers are abundant on these slopes.

82. C On these slopes, matter cycles and energy flows.

83. D The climax community usually is a rain forest.

84. A small group of people are stranded on a barren island with a thousand bushels of wheat and one cow. To survive for the greatest length of time, the people should

* A eat the cow, then eat the wheat.
B feed the wheat to the cow and drink the milk.
C feed the wheat to the cow, drink the milk, then eat the cow.
D drink the milk, eat the cow when milk production ceases, then eat the wheat.

85. Which of the following would reduce the amount of food available for human use?

A Increased production by producers
B Increased efficiency of energy use in herbivores eaten by humans
* C Increased number of consumer levels between producers and humans
D Decreased number of consumer levels between producers and humans.

86. Within any community, which would have the smallest total mass?

A Producers
B Primary consumers
* C Secondary consumers
D Decomposers

87. Which of the following is true about the ecosystem of New York City.

A It goes through a natural succession.
* B Its energy comes from other biological communities.
C It is a natural community.
D Its food webs are numerous.

88. The statement, "Everything is connected to everything else," expresses an understanding of

A populations.
* B ecosystems.
C individuals.
D species.
_____

The next two items are based on the figure below.

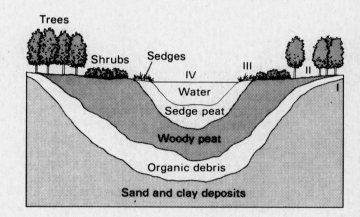

89. Which of the following concepts is represented by the figure?

A Matter flow
* B Succession
C Energy flow
D Spontaneous generation

90. The next layer deposited at Position III probably will be

A clay.
B water.
* C woody peat.
D sand.
_____

179

The next six items refer to the following diagram of a food web in a
freshwater pond.

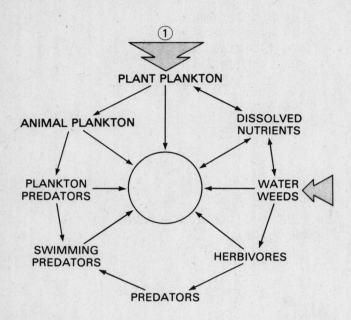

94. As indicated by the diagram, the
animal plankton are

   A producers.
* B primary consumers.
   C secondary consumers.
   D decomposers.

95. Which of the following organisms
would be represented by the center
circle?

   A Algae
   B Protozoa
   C Small arthropods
* D Bacteria

96. The principal organisms represented here as plant plankton would
be

* A diatoms.
   B protozoa.
   C rotifers.
   D water lilies.

91. The arrow at 1 most likely represents

   A primary consumers.
   B plants that give off oxygen.
   C animals that consume plant
      plankton.
* D light as the energy source.

92. The animal life in this community
would be damaged most by removal of
the

* A plant plankton.
   B animal plankton.
   C predators.
   D water weeds.

93. Which of the following are producers in this community?

   A Dissolved nutrients
* B Plant plankton
   C Animal plankton
   D The organism represented by
      the circle in the center

97. When farmers control pests by
spraying with insecticides, they are

   A reducing the amount of energy
      input into the ecosystem.
   B increasing the complexity of
      the food web.
   C increasing the possibility
      of eliminating dangerous
      species of animals.
* D reducing the food web to a
      simple food chain.

The next ten items are based on this diagram of a food web.

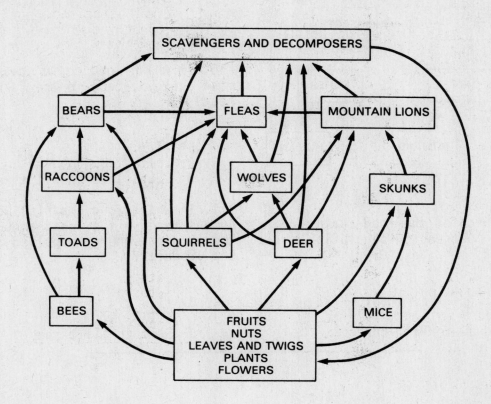

Use the Key to classify the statements.

KEY A Supported by the diagram
     B Contradicted by the diagram
     C Neither supported nor contra-
        dicted by the diagram

98. _B_ In this food web, raccoons
          are producers.

99. _A_ Bears feed on material that
          comes indirectly from fruits
          and flowers.

100. _A_ If deer hunting were stopped
          for one season, the wolf
          population would increase.

101. _C_ The greatest amount of food
          energy is consumed by the
          scavengers and decomposers.

102. _A_ Skunks are primary consumers.

103. _C_ If squirrels store larger
          supplies of nuts than usual,
          there will be a long and
          severe winter.

104. _A_ If hunters shoot more deer
          than usual, the squirrel
          population will be reduced.

105. _A_ Deer are primary consumers.

106. _A_ Bears can be classified as
          primary and secondary con-
          sumers.

107. _A_ The scavengers and decomposers
          help reduce organic material.

The next four items refer to the following diagram.

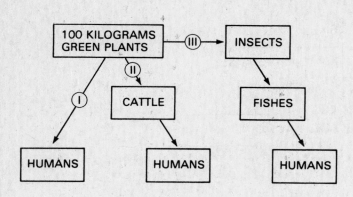

108. In which of the food chains would the most energy be available to humans?

*   A I
      B II
      C III
      D Equal for all three

109. Starving populations generally have diets like the food chain(s) in

*   A I.
      B II.
      C III.
      D II and III.

110. In which food chain does the most energy escape in the form of heat?

      A I
      B II
*   C III
      D Equal loss in all three

111. In which food chain(s) would humans receive the least amount of the original energy supplied by the producer?

      A I
      B II
*   C III
      D Same in all three

25 Challenges in Biology Today and Tomorrow

Consistent with the tone and purposes of Chapter 25, no multiple-choice test items are provided. Rather, the emphasis for both student evaluation and course evaluation should be placed on reflective discussion of the issues and ideas raised. Recall of specific facts and terms is less important than is an honest attempt to grapple with the complex problems facing our technological world. Also, it is important that students review what they have learned in their study of introductory biology--especially in terms of what science is and how scientists work.

Now is the time for each student to review his or her interests and performance and to make some plans for further exploration of the life sciences--whether as an interested and informed citizen working in some field that does not appear directly related to science or as one who wishes a vocation or avocation in science. In either case, the problems and potentials pointed out in this chapter represent but a few of the multifaceted areas of inquiry that scientists and citizens will face in the coming decades.

The following questions may help to get discussions going:

What are the consequences of population growth and its impact on freshwater supplies and living resources?

What is your community doing to provide fresh water and clean air for its population? What is your country doing? Your state?

What is the value of wildlife sanctuaries or national parks? What biological principles justify such areas?

How is quality of life for humans affected by the extinction of plant or animal species?

What social or personal values are affected by population control?

What are the consequences of uncontrolled population growth?

What means are available to control population growth?

What problems plague our attempts to provide each human being on earth an adequate food supply?

What ways are available to us to increase our food supply?

What are the effects of custom and religion on sources of food supply?

People who normally eat rice have been given wheat to sustain their lives. They will not eat the wheat. Can this be resolved?

People have tried to increase food supplies by changing food webs. What are the consequences of such actions?

To reduce air pollution, it has been suggested that automobiles be banned. What would be the results of such an action?

Has your community suggested or provided alternatives to the automobile? Have individuals in your community switched to alternative means of transportation? Why or why not?

When making decisions about resources and environmental quality, we sometimes choose to make compromises, or "trade-offs." To achieve a certain goal, we decide to sacrifice some other preference. Consider the values and consequences of the following pairs of trade-offs. Would you be willing to trade

- personal transportation via car for clean air?

- jobs in factories for clean water or air?

- higher prices for goods for pollution control devices in factories?

- limited access to national parks for preservation of natural ecosystems within the parks?

- reduced consumption of beef and other meat and increased consumption of plant protein for more efficient food production and more calories available for all people?

- small families for large families?

What other situations can you think of in which trade-offs like these must be made?

_____

Review the section "In Brief: Looking Back on This Course" on pages 738-739 of the text. Discuss each of the seven points individually. Cite examples from your own experience to illustrate each idea.

TOPICS FOR DISCUSSION

STRIP MINING IN THE APPALACHIANS

Read the following paragraphs. Then discuss the questions that follow.

Coal has been a major source of energy for the United States. The use of coal has declined dramatically in recent years, however. This has happened primarily because oil and natural gas have been available, inexpensive, and easy to obtain and ship. But many people believe coal will once again become a major energy source as supplies of other fossil fuels diminish and

costs rise. The Appalachian region, which has already been heavily mined, is believed to hold billions of tons of coal. The coal industries of Pennsylvania, West Virginia, Virginia, Alabama, Ohio, and Kentucky may flourish once again because of increasing demands for coal.

Many important economic and social consequences will result

from mining in Appalachia. Perhaps most obvious is the creation of jobs and much-needed income. In 1970, for example, 40 percent of the total earnings of Barbour County, West Virginia, resulted from coal mining jobs.

Before World War II, most of the coal taken from the hills of Appalachia was removed through shaft mines. Shaft mines can be (but seldom were) sealed. After the war, however, surface-mining operations became more popular. Surface mining, or strip mining, has much to recommend it.

Strip mines can be put into operation much more quickly than can deep mines. And one worker on a strip-mine operation can extract as much coal each day as three miners in a shaft. Strip mining results in little waste. Most of the coal is removed. In contrast, about half the coal in a deep mine is left behind as insurance against cave-ins. Other advantages are: strip mines are far safer than underground mines and they even have a history of fewer labor problems. Add to all this the estimate that 20 to 30 percent of our best coal deposits are close to the surface, and one can establish a very convincing argument in favor of strip mining.

Although the methods of surface-mining operations vary, depending primarily on the slope of the land, the end results are similar. The land is denuded of vegetation and its topography is changed. But do the effects of strip mining end there?

To follow the chain of impacts associated with strip mining, one must ask, "What are the effects of deforestation and alteration of land forms?" To simplify the picture, one can identify at least four major results of the mining operation.

First is the silting of streams.

When the cover of vegetation is removed, soil is washed into streams. Second, chemical runoff from the land can be observed and measured. Streams are discolored by yellow and red iron compounds and other pollutants. Third, changes in topography result in the formation of new ponds and lakes. The holes that remain when the land is removed fill with water, producing semipermanent or permanent ponds. Fourth, removing the vegetation destroys food and habitats for animal populations.

Thus, four major effects of strip-mining operations have been identified. But the chain of events does not stop here. These *effects* become *causes* of still other *effects*.

First, consider silting. Studies of silting in Appalachian streams revealed that silting reduces the water-carrying capacity of upland streams. Massive volumes of silt are carried downstream to larger tributaries and finally are deposited in major rivers. These deposits fill in the river bottoms. Raising the bottom of a river often causes flooding, which can damage property and endanger human health and safety. Silting also interferes with fish reproduction. And it kills small bottom-dwelling insects and crustaceans, a major source of food for bottom-feeding fish. These effects reduce fish populations and populations of animals that eat fish, such as raccoons, grebes, loons, and mink.

Now consider another effect-- acid mine runoff. Iron compounds washed from newly exposed rocks enter the streams. Some are oxidized into harmless compounds. Others, however, are changed to sulfuric acid, a lethal compound that can cause massive fish kills. Scientists have found that certain bacteria in the water actually aggravate the problem. In the process of drawing their energy from inorganic compounds, these bacteria increase the acid content of the water by as much as 400 percent. Acid kills not only fish but aquatic plants as well. Once again, the chain of effects causes still other effects. Food-chain relationships are disturbed, and fish populations are reduced, with corresponding reductions in animal populations.

The next effect of strip mining would seem to be a good one. Coal company representatives have sometimes argued that stripping actually increases fishing and recreation through the formation of ponds. Unfortunately, this assertion seems to be more hope than fact. Few strip-mine ponds have shallow areas where fish can breed. In those that do, the shallow areas become so crowded that fry (young fish) are too numerous and their growth is stunted.

The fourth effect causes a much simpler and more obvious series of occurrences. But the magnitude and importance of the impact may be as

great as with other effects. Stripping the land removes food sources and natural habitats of animal populations. The "simple" effect is the reduction of all animal populations, not just those that live on fish.

(Adapted from BSCS, 1977, *Biological Science: Interaction of Experiments and Ideas*, Prentice-Hall, Englewood Cliffs, N. J.)

Discussion Questions

1. *How important is the extinction of a fish species when compared with the benefits of industrialization and economic growth?*

2. *What has civilization lost or gained when millions of fish die, but millions of kilowatt hours of electricity are generated?*

3. *How much environmental quality should we sacrifice to supply our cultural, social, and economic needs for fuels?*

ENERGY CONSUMPTION AND CONSERVATION

Read the following paragraphs. Then discuss the questions that follow.

Human activities require great quantities of energy. In an earlier time, the only energy people used was food energy--the energy of the sun that is trapped in plants. With advancing civilization, energy use grew far beyond basic food requirements. Today, most of the things we do and all of the products we use rely on a considerable energy input.

Virtually all of that input comes from one source--fossil fuels. Fossil fuels are coal, oil, and natural gas--the remains of plants and animals that lived millions of years

ago. The problem is that fossil fuels will run out--sooner or later. Should these sources of energy cease to be available, the things we do and the way we do them would change significantly. How great the change would be depends on a number of related questions. We would need to answer such questions as, "Can another source of energy be used for the same purpose?" or "Can some other activities be as useful and satisfying."

In an attempt to solve energy problems, the federal government recently instituted a variety of laws and policies. The adoption of a nationwide speed limit of 55 miles per hour is one of several actions taken to meet severe gas shortages in the summer of 1973. Some of these actions, such as adopting the speed limit, were mandatory. Others, such as the "Don't be fuelish" campaign, encouraged voluntary citizen action.

Some political or legal energy decisions have led to clashes between governments at various levels. Questions of energy development in the western states, for example, are still open to conflicts of jurisdiction. And decisions about such potential developments as the production of shale oil in Colorado affect not only Coloradoans but also residents of other states and Mexico. These areas rely on water from the Colorado River. The political and legal effects extend far outside national boundaries. The now infamous Arab oil embargo has emphasized the extent of international energy dependency.

(Adapted from BSCS, 1977, *Energy and Society: Investigations in Decision Making*, Hubbard Scientific Co., Northbrook, Illinois.)

Discussion Questions

1.   *The use of fossil fuels accounts for 95 percent of our nation's total energy use. What do you think would happen if fossil fuels suddenly were not available?*

2.   *Discuss the pros and cons of problem solving through laws versus voluntary citizen action.*

3.   *In what ways are energy problems of community, state, national, and international concern?*

4.   *What are some of the trade-offs involved in deciding to develop an energy resource like the oil shales of Colorado?*

5.   *Review the Science at Work feature "Tragedy of the Commons" on page 708 of the text. How do Hardin's ideas apply to the development of energy resources like oil shale?*

HEALTH CARE RESPONSIBILITY

Read the following paragraphs. Then discuss the questions that follow.

The major health problems now confronting industrialized nations are not infectious diseases, as in the early part of this century. In 1900, six of the ten leading causes of death in the United States were either infectious diseases or disabilities related to them. Before the nineteenth century, "only about three out of every ten newborn infants lived beyond the age of 25. Of the seven who died, two or three never reached their first birthday, and five or six died before they were six years of age."[1] Today, however, in developed countries, influenza, pneumonia, and certain diseases of early infancy are the only infectious disorders among the ten major causes of death.[2,3] In these countries, fewer than one in twenty children die before reaching adulthood.

Health specialists do not agree about the factors that reduced infectious diseases. Some say that medical intervention, in the form of immunization and treatment, is the reason. Others claim that most medical interventions were ineffective before sulfa drugs, antibiotics, and improved vaccines were developed. And they feel that, even with widespread use, those techniques were not very effective. This second group claims that "reduced contact with microorganisms"--achieved by improved sanitation--has been responsible for the reduction in infectious disease.[1] They also feel that improved nutrition has led to increased resistance to infectious organisms. And they point out that declining birthrates in many nations have reduced the pressure on food resources and sanitation. Regardless of which position is more accurate, the fact is that the advanced nations now face a new class of health problems.

The diseases that now head the list are heart disease, cancer, stroke, lung disease, diabetes, arteriosclerosis, and cirrhosis. Often, these are associated with the fact that people live longer than they used to. They also are diseases of lifestyle. Many of the risk factors for such disorders are known to be functions of the environment created by industrialized societies. These may be either physical--environmental pollution--or emotional--stress and anxiety. Personal habits such as sedentary living, poor eating habits, smoking, and alcohol consumption also contribute to the problem.

Neither the environment nor a person's lifestyle operates in a vacuum. Each interacts with the other. In addition, each interacts with the unique genetic makeup of every individual. Thus, when one tries to establish a method to assure good health for everyone, genetics must be considered.

Health care methods will be different for persons of different ages, sexes, or life circumstances. They also will be dependent on each individual's genetic makeup. For example, an athlete will have different health care needs than will a person whose greatest talents are outside the field of sports. Health care will be different for a diabetic person from that of a person who does not have diabetes. Nevertheless, by thinking about their lifestyles and making informed decisions based on an understanding of genetic differences, individuals can learn to improve their health.

Discussion Questions

1. *Experts believe that many adult health problems actually begin in the teenage years. As teenagers, say the experts, people learn poor health habits, such as smoking and alcohol consumption. Continuing these habits then leads to serious health problems later in life.*

A person's environment includes the emotional setting as well as the physical surroundings. Discuss some of the conditions in the teenage environment that might cause a young person to engage in "health-compromising behavior."

2. *Many health-care issues present difficult ethical and legal questions. Cigarette smoking is known to be directly related to lung cancer and heart disease. Smokers who have these disorders cost society large sums of money in lost work days, increased hospital costs, and higher insurance premiums. Should society have the right to ban harmful habits such as smoking? Should government support, through programs like Medicaid and Medicare, be denied to people who continue to practice harmful habits?*

3. *Geneticists believe that soon it will be possible to determine whether*

a person is genetically predisposed to a certain type of chronic disorder. Should a person who may be genetically predisposed to heart disease be prohibited from becoming an air traffic controller? Or should that person not be allowed, by law, to use butter because it contains unsaturated fats?

Researchers have found that a number of physical and chemical agents used in industry are teratogenic--they can cause birth defects. Does industry or the government have the right to prevent women of childbearing age from working in situations where they might be exposed to these substances? Should the use of such agents be prohibited? What would happen if, for example, mercury no longer could be used to make thermometers or fluorescent lights?

4. *Some health-care professionals feel that people should assume more responsibility for their own health. They believe that most people rely too heavily on doctors and hospitals for health maintenance. Do you think these assumptions are correct? What aspects of the health-care system encourage or discourage personal responsibility for health care?*

What kinds of things do you do that help to maintain your good health? What other steps might you take? What kinds of illnesses might you avoid by improving your personal health-care practices?

References

1. McKeown, T. "The Determinants of Health." *Human Nature*, 1(4): April, 1978.

2. Dingle, J. H. "The Ills of Man." *Scientific American*, 299(3): September, 1973.

3. U. S. Dept. of Health, Education, and Welfare. *Health, United States, 1976-2977.* DHEW Publication Number (HRA) 77-1232, Hyattsville, Md., 1977.

Teaching Notes

Teaching Notes

Teaching Notes

Teaching Notes

Teaching Notes

Teaching Notes

Teaching Notes